DAILY WORD

for the Spirit

50 Stories of Faith, Prayer and Inspiration

DAILY WORD

for the Spirit

50 Stories of Faith, Prayer and Inspiration

Colleen Zuck

Editor

Unity Village, Missouri

DAILY WORD for the Spirit

First Edition 2010

Third printing 2012

Unity Books are available at special discounts for bulk purchases for study groups, book clubs, sales promotions, book signings or fundraising. To place an order, call the Unity Customer Care Department at 1-866-236-3571 or email *wholesaleaccts@unityonline.org*

Cover design: Jenny Hahn

Interior design: The Covington Group, Kansas City, MO

Library of Congress Control Number: 2010924843

ISBN: 978-0-87159-283-5

Canada BN 13252 0933 RT

Contents

CONTENTS

Introduction

"Tell me a story!" As children—before we learned to read—we may have often made that request of our parents or other adults. Did your spirit and imagination soar, like mine, when told stories from the Bible: Moses stretching out his hand and parting the sea, Ruth gleaning grain from the fields of Boaz, Jesus healing the blind and feeding the multitude?

Some of my earliest memories are of listening to true-life stories told by my grandmother, mother and father. Through their stories, I caught glimpses of how their lives were years ago: I felt the thrill my father must have felt as he rode full speed on the back of his horse, and I cringed when he told how he was knocked from his horse as he tried to grab an overhanging limb, imitating cowboys in the movies he loved. I was refreshed as my mother described how as a young girl she drank cold, clear water from a spring near her mountain home on a warm summer day. My grandmother told me about her father: He was such an engaging storyteller that those who were bedfast for a time often requested that he sit with them. He described events so vividly, that, for a time, he took their mind off what was wrong with them, and they made a quick recovery.

As I learned to read, I allowed myself to be transported to situations and places where neither time nor space could limit my experiences of excitement and discovery. Over the years I have read

1

biographies and autobiographies. I was fascinated by people's stories. They not only entertained, they also informed. Whenever I attended a seminar, workshop or retreat, I was inspired by the stories of other people: how they attained success, found peace of mind, and considered themselves prosperous.

I never want to underestimate the importance that our shared stories can be to one another. They create bonds between two people and among groups of people—families and friends, congregants and communities. One person can share a life story or an event that others relate to and are helped by.

Years ago when I first attended a Weight Watchers® meeting, the first person to greet me was a tall, slim woman. Silently I thought: *I doubt that she was ever even 10 pounds overweight.* During a later meeting, this woman shared her story: She had lost over 100 pounds and kept it off for several years. I was amazed—and embarrassed that I had not appreciated her success until I heard her story. She inspired me to get serious about meeting my goal.

In my nearly 25 years as editor of *Daily Word,* some of my most rewarding experiences were learning how people had found *Daily Word*—and how it had helped them at a time when there seemed no other place to turn to.

One person wrote to tell me that several years ago as she stepped off a curb, she saw a *Daily Word* lying in the gutter. She picked it up, and after carefully reading it, knew that she had found the inspiration she needed to move her life in a more positive direction. *Daily Word* continued to encourage her on her spiritual journey.

Many people have found *Daily Word* in waiting rooms of doctors' offices or the family rooms of hospitals. A person who has been helped by *Daily Word* leaves a copy as a helping hand to another. I learned this personally when I met a mother and daughter on a Unity cruise in 2009. These two women were always smiling, as if they didn't have a care in the world. One evening the mother mentioned that being on the cruise was a gift to her daughter, who was celebrating her 50th birthday. I was puzzled when the daughter said, "I never thought I would make it to 50." The mother explained that her daughter had stage-four cancer and that 20 years ago this mother had found *Daily Word* at a hospital where her daughter was first treated for cancer. *Daily Word* had gotten them through some very challenging times. These two women were such an inspiration to me. They were living in the moment, enjoying life and one another as if that was all that mattered. And I understood that, indeed, this was a truth we all can live by no matter what is happening.

Daily Word has a life of its own—meeting people as they are with a message of inspiration and prayer support. One day I was reading through a stack of "good reports"—readers telling us how much *Daily Word* meant to them, how they were helped by a certain message—which is a goldmine of information for an editor. The third letter I read this one morning was an apology, a confession of guilt. A *Daily Word* had been delivered to this person's mailbox by mistake. She was apologizing because she had read mail that wasn't addressed to her, but she added that she needed *Daily Word*. She had returned that issue to the right mailbox and was ordering her own subscription. I couldn't help but think that a mail carrier's mistake was really a spiritual intervention that had turned this woman from feelings of despair to hope. No, there are no mistakes in Spirit.

One sentence can sometimes tell a great story. As editor, I usually didn't handle order forms for *Daily Word* subscriptions—unless there was something sent specifically for my attention. At first I didn't see anything on a renewal form that came to me, and then I noticed something written on the bottom corner. I read the clear handwriting: "I turned 101 this year!" Although I had never met this person, when I saw that she was renewing for *three years*, I knew she was a person full of life, hope and great expectations. How she lifted my spirits and reminded me that at the age of 94, Charles Fillmore, co-founder of Unity, wrote: "I fairly sizzle with zeal and enthusiasm and spring forth with a mighty faith to do that which is mine to do."

Over the years as editor of *Daily Word*, I had the privilege of interviewing hundreds of people and writing stories from many of those interviews. All the people and circumstances were different, but there were familiar threads that made up the fabric of each story: faith that they sustained through prayer, an understanding that they were spiritual beings going through human experiences, and the unquestioning belief that the spirit of God within them was greater than any challenge they could ever experience. They overcame challenges of health or circumstances. They accepted God-given opportunities and claimed their rightful heritage as whole and happy creations of God.

I have interviewed famous people and those who had never been in the public eye; all were gracious and willing to share what seemed to be personal tragedies but turned into triumphs.

I cried with some and laughed with others. I learned from some how reading *Daily Word* had saved their lives, pointed them in the right direction, or lifted them out of depression.

We all have our own amazing stories. It's when we open the windows of our souls and let others into our world that we inspire, teach by example, and give gifts of unequaled value and meaning.

Choosing just a few of my favorite *Daily Word* stories was difficult. The final 50 stories collected in this book hold special meaning for me, and I hope they do for you also. As added features, I share some thoughts—a "Preview"—about the person to set up each story. After each one, there is a "Postscript," some added, updated information about the person.

Stories like those featured in this book allow us a view into the depths of others' souls so that we are inspired and offered direction on our own journeys of life. Prepare yourself to be blessed by these tales of giving and receiving love, of forgiving and being forgiven, of healing and helping others to heal. Through sharing of our own soul journeys with one another, we experience "Spirit bearing witness with our spirit that we are children of God" (Romans 8:16). We understand that as we give expression to the power and presence of God within us, we overcome challenges; we answer the call of Spirit to be all that we were created to be. I believe the selection of the stories in this book offers you all this and even more.

PROSPERITY

I open my heart to the goodness of God.

True prosperity is more than financial well-being or the accumulation of material things. I am most prosperous when I acknowledge God's goodness in every area of my life and give thanks for the blessings that come my way each day.

With a prosperity consciousness, I give thanks for all the ways I experience God's goodness. Family and friends are rich blessings in my life. Personal skills help me find right employment and advancement. Humor, wisdom and energy enrich my days. I realize true prosperity as I open my heart to the goodness of God.

But when the goodness and loving kindness of God our Savior appeared, he saved us, not because of any works of righteousness that we had done, but according to his mercy, through the water of rebirth and renewal by the Holy Spirit.—Titus 3:4-5

Preview

My mother taught me that giving and receiving love blesses a person with more prosperity than any amount of money or possessions ever could. She didn't lecture me about love; she was an example—every day of her life—of the good that love can do when expressed in small and large matters.

How much love does a heart hold or is capable of expressing? How important is it to put our love into action for the sole purpose of blessing others? I believe there is no act of love that is too insignificant to touch the lives of others in ways that benefit them in the moment and for a lifetime.

Heart of Love

By Colleen Zuck

Most Missouri winters offer a diversity of weather: warm and cold days, and dry and wet spells. In fact, those born and raised here advise new residents and visitors, "If you don't like the weather in Missouri, stick around because it will change tomorrow."

Just before Christmas in 1954 (I believe that was the year) it was bitterly cold. Snow filled the ditches and low spots in the ground of our hilltop community. The neighborhood took on a surreal look of black and white, a contrast of earth and snow. Our house, with an acre and a half of land, was at a point where the urban scene shifted into a rural one.

This was the Christmas when I learned the difference between material wealth and spiritual wealth: I experienced what it was to give from the abundance of God's love that was within me.

A Helping Hand

My mother was the manager of our neighborhood grocery store, but more than that she was the caring heart of our community. She was a champion of recycling long before it became popular. Clothes were passed down in our extended family. I remember being relieved when my feet outgrew some of the clunky shoes my cousins and even my aunts passed along. Mother also collected toys for the children in our neighborhood, often cleaning dolls and washing and ironing the dolls' clothes.

But back to this cold morning just before Christmas when I was about 13 years old. Mother called me into the kitchen and began to pull canisters out of the cabinets. She directed me to the refrigerator, saying, "We need milk for the gravy." I questioned what we were doing since we had already eaten breakfast. Then she explained she had learned that the family down the road from us was without food. "Jesus fed 5,000 with five loaves and fishes, and we ought to find enough food in this kitchen to feed a family of seven."

Mother began heaping flour into a large crockery bowl. After she had added and mixed other ingredients, she rolled the dough out on a floured board. She then pressed out big, round biscuits—enough to feed a dozen people!

Sliding the biscuit pan into the oven, she began making a huge pot of milk gravy, saying, "I need your help carrying this food over to Kitty and her children."

I immediately felt embarrassed about taking biscuits and gravy to this family. What if they didn't like this kind of food? What if they felt embarrassed—about not having enough?

Within 30 minutes, Mother and I were walking down the road to Kitty's house. Mother was in front carrying the pot of steaming hot gravy, and I reluctantly followed behind with the pan of biscuits, covered by a clean dish towel.

When Mother knocked at the door, a young boy about 7 years old answered. "I thought you might enjoy some biscuits and gravy," Mother announced with all the ease she did when passing a bowl of food at our family table.

As we entered the house, I was struck by how cold it was inside. There was no heat. Steam flowed from the pot of gravy and billowed up to the living room ceiling. Five other children appeared in the room followed by their mother.

An Abundance of Love

One girl, several years younger than me, looked at the pan of biscuits I was holding and then looked into my face as though she were looking at an angel. I was seeing myself through her eyes, and I felt so good about the person whom *she* was seeing. I knew that's who I wanted to be. I felt like an angel, not because of *me* but because the abundance of God's love being shared by two families filled that small home.

During the walk back home, Mother and I were quiet, but I felt warm and happy. From that day on I enjoyed helping Mother share her heart of love by giving what we had to give, knowing that no gesture of caring and no gift given in honor of God's love were too insignificant or small.

Years later when I found Unity, I understood that Mother had a prosperity consciousness that was so much a part of the Unity teachings. Although she didn't have much, materially, she expressed the love of God abundantly.

Because Mother now has Alzheimer's, she doesn't always know how to feed herself. Often when I am feeding her, she lets me know with a word or gesture that she wants me to share her food and even to eat first.

Yes, God's love expressed by Mother is stronger than Alzheimer's and any other adverse condition or circumstance. What prosperous people we are when we love and are willing to be loved.

Postscript

My mother was also my teacher, my friend and my greatest supporter. She grew up in what most would consider extreme poverty. Yet having less didn't dampen her passion to give to others. With only a third-grade education, she had a wisdom that exceeded "book learning." As I was growing up, Mother's nightly ritual was to tuck me in bed and then, down on her knees beside my bed, she would pray with me. Remembering these prayer times with Mother blesses me to this day.

In 2007 at age 97, Mother experienced what the doctors called *heart failure*, but I knew that her heart of love never failed. I was at her bedside, praying with her, telling her how much all her family loved her and thanking her for being a wonderful mother. I told her that her family was okay and that she could go on to her rest. And as if she was waiting to hear that, she took her last breath and rested her heart of love. I know that her family and everyone who ever met her would agree that she left this world with a lot more love than there was before she came into it. This is something each of us can do; we can prosper the world with love.

2

LET GO, LET GOD

The love of God unites my loved ones and me in a circle of love.

I know that worrying about my loved ones and creating "what if" scenarios in my mind are not going to do them or me any good. So I let go of worry and know that the best results happen as we let God guide us.

I let go and let God be in charge by taking myself a step further. Instead of just knowing the truth, I live it. As I do this, I focus on creating an atmosphere of peace and contentment around me. By letting go, I am opening a door to peace and inviting the unlimited love of God to comfort me.

Even when my loved ones are out of my sight, the spirit of God is our vital connection. We are as close to one another as a prayer. Wherever my loved ones may be, the spirit of God is within them. At this very moment, divine love is surrounding and embracing them and uniting us in a circle of love.

Have faith in God.—Mark 11:22

Preview

I often wonder about the people I see while shopping at a mall or sitting in the waiting area at an airport: *What's your story?* We know only sketches here and there of what's going on in the lives of those we see at work or in class daily. More than likely, we haven't a clue of the ups and downs of those we see during our regular shopping day at the grocery store or appointment at the hairdresser's.

Both Gardiner Rapelye and I worked in the same Silent Unity building for several years, but in different areas of service. We had chatted on occasion while riding the elevator or passing in hallways. One day another co-worker told me a miraculous story about Gardiner's son Tanner, and the next time I saw Gardiner, I asked him if he would share his story with the *Daily Word* family. He did, and each time I read "Surrendering All to God," I receive a blessing. As you turn the page, I believe you will find a story that will inspire you as it did me.

Surrendering All to God

By Rev. Gardiner Rapelye Jr.

When my sons Tanner and Beau were 8 and 14, their mother and I divorced, and I started a new life as a single parent. During those early years, I had gotten used to the usual bumps and scrapes that happen to kids. However, at 11 p.m. on September 17, 2005, I received a call that turned my world upside down. Twenty-four-year-old Tanner had fallen from the fourth-floor balcony of his apartment in Kansas City, Missouri.

Rushing off to the hospital from my home 20 miles away, I made several urgent calls. I phoned Beau, in California, and his mother, in North Carolina. I called Silent Unity, and I called my prayer partner from ministerial school, Rev. Debbie Taylor.

Earlier that day, Tanner and his roommate had helped me pack boxes for a Gulf Coast relief drive at Unity Temple on the Plaza in Kansas City. The boxes were being sent to people who were made homeless by Hurricane Katrina. Tanner had said, "Dad, I really want to do more of this." We had lunch and then went our separate ways. By that evening, a beautiful afternoon with my son had turned into a horrific crisis.

When I arrived at the hospital emergency unit, a doctor took me into a small consultation room. "Your son may survive," he said, "but if he does, he may be totally nonfunctioning." When he told me I couldn't go in to be with Tanner, I said, "I'm an ordained minister and I can handle this. I've got to be by his side."

My Little Boy

When Tanner was born, I was in the delivery room. As soon as the doctor delivered Tanner, she handed him to me. Tanner grabbed my thumb, and I remember thinking, "This little boy is going to help me." Now I knew that as never before I needed to be there for him.

Finally, I was allowed in to see him. Tanner was in a coma, his pelvis was fractured, and a broken rib had damaged his spleen. Before they did a tracheotomy and placed Tanner on life support, I tried to straighten the oxygen tube going into his nose. Even though he was in a coma, I thought I might be able to do something that could make him feel more comfortable. One of the doctors who was watching said, "This isn't a movie. There's not going to be any pretty music, and there may be no happy ending." "Well," I affirmed, "I'm in prayer knowing that we are going to see a happy ending and that he is going to be just fine."

Hitting the ground after a four-story fall, Tanner aspirated the contents of his stomach into his lungs, which caused severe burns throughout the interior of his lungs. His brain was swollen to the capacity of his skull, but it was the damage to his lungs that soon threatened to take his life.

Twice the doctor prescribed a risky steroid treatment. "You have a choice here," he said. "You can either watch him crash and burn or you can let us try to save his life with a steroid treatment. But know that he may not survive the treatment itself."

I thought, Okay, we are either going to be planning a funeral or for long-term care, and I'll do whatever I'm called to do. It was so clear from that moment on that I had to surrender, get out of the way, and listen to divine guidance.

Beau flew in from California, and the boys' mother flew in from North Carolina. Tanner had at least one of us by his side at all times. I was comforted to know the prayers of Silent Unity were going on 24 hours a day, every day. Debbie started a prayer chain for Tanner, and we received cards from people all over the world, telling us they were praying for him.

We never left Tanner unattended, and I believe that during the eight weeks he was in a coma, he somehow sensed that we were there, pulling for him. I said the "Prayer for Protection" for him over and over again, believing each time that he heard me:

Tanner,
The light of God surrounds you;
The love of God enfolds you;
The power of God protects you;
The presence of God watches over you.
Wherever you are, God is!

Tanner's recovery was a very slow process. The first indication I saw that he was coming out of the coma was when a tiny bit of one side of his lip turned up, as if he were trying to smile. Then he started moving one of his little fingers. We cheered him on, hoping and praying that he was really coming back. The doctors were very cautious, saying, "Don't get too excited about any of this."

On the other hand, prayers for him continued, and his progress steadily improved. We prayed, Silent Unity prayed around the clock, and people all over the world prayed. Tanner became more active and coherent. He was able to work the call button, keeping his nurses busy.

One morning when I arrived early at the hospital, Tanner had the TV remote in his hand. "Dad, look!" he said. I looked up and saw that he had The Worship Network on—beautiful scenes, lovely music, scriptures and inspirational messages that continued 24 hours a day. He had been awake all night watching the program.

Tanner went from 250 to 140 pounds while he was in the hospital. He had to learn everything all over again: how to move his hands, arms and legs. He had to learn how to walk, talk, and take care of himself.

When he came out of the hospital, Tanner stayed with me for two weeks. At first I felt as nervous as if I had a newborn in the house. I would listen for any noise he would make: Was he coughing? Turning over in the bed? He'd been taken care of by nurses and doctors for so long, I wasn't sure if I could do it. Tanner improved so rapidly that he really didn't require much care.

Beau quit his job in California, and he and Tanner moved in together. They lived right across the street from me. We had this family-compound thing going on for a while, which was very comforting.

Finding the Good

When Tanner fell four stories to the ground, he landed on a patch of grass and dirt that was about three feet wide by five feet long. That patch of ground, surrounded by rock, brick, stone steps and metal fences, had just been watered. After his fall, an imprint of Tanner was visible on that patch of grass and dirt. If he had fallen in any other spot, more than likely, he would not have survived.

To this day, I don't know how or why Tanner fell; Tanner doesn't remember how the fall happened. What I do know is that Spirit has great plans for this young man. When I look at him, I thank God he survived so many surgeries and procedures. He mended beautifully. As I like to say: "He's alive, awake, alert, enthusiastic and prospering." He's working now as a financial planner. His high-school sweetheart, Sara, came back into his life as a result of the accident, and they are engaged.

My sons and I have always been incredibly close, but now we're even closer. I've learned that when I pray and look for the good in every situation, I find it. I also know that what God leads me to, God leads me through. Whether it is a crisis or an opportunity for good, I'm to get out of the way and surrender all to God.

Postscript

In 2001, after a successful career as an interior designer, Gardiner Rapelye Jr. made the decision to go into the ministry. He was ordained as a Unity minister in June of 2005, three months before his son Tanner's accident.

Tanner and Sara, his high-school sweetheart, were married November 1, 2008, and resided in Prairie Village, Kansas. Tanner is planning on speaking to other young college-age people about his accident and the challenges that arise from drug and alcohol abuse.

Gardiner reports that when the article was published in *Daily Word*, he began hearing from people he had not heard from in years. He was also contacted by people he didn't know who were helped by reading his story. "All of which," he says, "speaks volumes of how *Daily Word* reaches out to people."

At the time of the publication of this book, Gardiner had retired from Silent Unity and moved to Maine to take care of property he and the boys had inherited from his father. He says: "I am looking forward to once again living close enough to spend time with my family—especially Sunday mornings, attending church together, and at anytime, enjoying a meal together."

3

FORGIVE

Thank You, God, for Your loving, forgiving spirit within all.

Dear God, I turn to Your gentle presence today in a spirit of forgiveness. I invite You to guide and inspire me as I release any past hurts or perceived slights initiated by others or by myself.

I forgive anyone I may have held resentment toward, and I affirm and give thanks for Your healing, forgiving presence within each person. May forgiveness be complete within every heart and mind so that the relationships of both friends and family can be valued and meaningful to all.

God, I release any need for a particular outcome and remain open to the spirit of forgiveness within me and within others.

So when you are offering your gift at the altar, if you remember that your brother or sister has something against you, leave your gift there before the altar and go; first be reconciled to your brother or sister, and then come and offer your gift.—
Matthew 5:23-24

Preview

When I listened to Imaculée Ilibagiza tell her story, I heard pain and sadness in her voice. She had lost many family members during the Rwandan genocide. As her story unfolded, I could hear something else emerging in the sound of her soft, gentle voice. I believe it was a balm of forgiveness that was continuing to soothe her wounded heart.

Imaculée awakened in me a greater realization of the healing power released in acts of forgiveness. I was amazed but understood why this young woman chose to do what she did after learning of the annihilation of her family.

As you read her story, I believe you will hear a strength and faith that perhaps you have never before heard.

The Healing Power of Forgiveness

By Immaculée Ilibagiza

In the spring of 1994, I was a college student, home for Easter. As the protected daughter of loving parents and cherished sister of three wonderful brothers, I was enjoying life in my homeland of Rwanda.

Although we were of the Tutsi ethnic minority in a country run by an extremist Hutu regime, we could not have imagined the genocide that was about to begin. On April 6, the president of Rwanda, a Hutu, was killed in a plane crash, and Tutsi rebels were accused of shooting down the plane. My family, along with millions of other Tutsis, knew there would be retaliation.

We were ordered not to leave the country, and business as usual stopped. When the killing of Tutsis began, my parents sent me to hide in the home of Pastor Simeon Nzabahimana, a sympathetic Hutu. Different members of my family hid in several other places.

Pastor Simeon took in seven more Tutsi women. Our hiding place was the small second bathroom of his house. Eight of us were wedged into that 3- by 4-foot space. We would spend the next three months there. Occasionally—and only at night—we would come out of the bathroom and lie down in the adjoining room. There was a window in this room, so we didn't dare stay there in the daytime.

To keep his two children from discovering us, the pastor told them that the small bathroom was locked and that the key to unlock it had been lost. The other women and I listened to a radio that Pastor Simeon had placed outside the bathroom door. The BBC reported daily of the growing number of Tutsis who had been brutally killed. Many entire families were wiped out.

For three months, not daring to make a noise that might cause us to be discovered, we women used hand signals to talk to one another. Once a day or sometimes once every other day, Pastor Simeon brought us food and water. We flushed the toilet only when we would hear the other toilet in the house being flushed.

Hutu killers came to the house and searched. During the search, I silently prayed and said the Rosary. I held my breath when I heard the men approach the bathroom door. I believe it was nothing less than a miracle that they turned and left, never attempting to open the door. Knowing that they would return, I begged the pastor to move a large armoire in front of the bathroom door. He did and then stacked suitcases on top of it.

Listening from the silence of the bathroom to the BBC radio reports of the genocide that was happening, I grew angrier each day. I spent hours imagining that I was a Tutsi soldier, taking revenge on the Hutu killers. My anger grew to the point that I became upset with myself. I questioned how I could pray to God for help when I was so angry. I believed that someday I would be able to walk out of that cramped bathroom and start living my life again. But I began to question myself: How could I have a life if I were still angry and feeling the hurt that hating others caused me?

I prayed and read the Bible, gaining a better understanding that all people are children of God. I accepted that those who were doing the killing didn't understand the truth of this. They had been blinded by anger and hate. I knew that in order to continue with life once I was free, I had to forgive.

Once the Hutus were defeated, the genocide stopped, and the other women and I were rescued. I learned from others about my family—who had survived and who had not. All—except one brother who was out of the country—had been killed. My mother, father, two brothers, grandparents, aunts, uncles and cousins had perished. Many of my friends and neighbors were also gone. Later we learned that nearly 1 million people had been killed in the genocide—most victims were Tutsis, but some were moderate Hutu sympathizers.

Forgiving the Unforgivable

I was told that one of our former Hutu neighbors was the leader of a gang that had killed my mother and my brother. When I heard that he was being held in a local prison, I decided to go see him. I didn't know what I would do when I saw him face to face.

When a guard brought the man from his cell, I hardly recognized this former neighbor, the father of children I had known as I was growing up. His hair was disheveled, and bits of food clung to his unshaven face. He stared at me defiantly. I wanted to be free of hatred because I had seen what the hatred of this man and other Hutus had done. When I quietly but sincerely said three short words, "I forgive you," I felt a peace sweep over my soul. The man's defiant look melted away, and he bowed his head. I'm sure it was in shame for what he had done.

As I walked out of the prison, the Tutsi man who ran the prison turned to me in anger. "How could you forgive him?" he said. The man had lost his children during the genocide. A year later, I met him again, and he told me that I had changed his life. He had been so full of hate and anger that he was miserable. When he saw that I could forgive and move on with my life after all I had been through and lost, he knew this was also what he wanted to do.

With the healing of my own heart, I was able to start anew in the United States. I wanted to reach out to help heal the hearts of others, to help heal my homeland. I told my story in the books *Left to Tell* and *Led By Faith*. I founded the Left to Tell Charitable Fund to assist children left orphaned by the genocide. Through the fund, many children have been placed in homes.

Everyone goes through difficulties in life. It's important that we don't give up. I believe that it's only when we have the peace of mind that forgiveness brings us that we are able to move on to live our lives fully.

Postscript

Four years after the tragedy in her homeland, Immaculée Ilibagiza immigrated to the United States. In 2007 Immaculée was awarded the Mahatma Gandhi International Award for Peace and Reconciliation. She has written three books: *Left to Tell*, *Led by Faith* and *Our Lady of Kibeho.*

Immaculée continues to spread her message of peace, faith and forgiveness throughout the world, raising money for her Left to Tell Charitable Fund, which directly benefits the children orphaned by the Rwandan genocide. For more information about Immaculée, visit *www.immaculee.com.*

4

RENEWED

Renewed by the power and presence of God, I am healed.

Continuing to know and to speak the truth that I am whole and well may be difficult when I am experiencing a health challenge.

Yet I am encouraged to know this truth as I read the Bible. One story offered there tells of a woman who had been ill for 12 years. The doctors were unable to cure her, and her resources were all but spent. In spite of all this, she had faith. In a crowd one day, following Jesus, she reached out and touched his cloak, believing that she would be made well. Through the power and presence of God, she was healed.

Divine healing power is actively expressing renewal throughout my being right now. Laying aside all doubt, I affirm that through the presence and power of God, I am healed.

He said to her, "Daughter, your faith has made you well; go in peace, and be healed of your disease." —Mark 5:34

Preview

We only have to turn to a newspaper or turn on the TV or radio to learn the bad news of our world. Yet there is so much good news to share.

The following story was published in *Daily Word* after Unity minister Rev. Bill Englehart contacted me with some good news. Jeffery Perry, a member of Rev. Englehart's church, had been healed of cancer after doctors said he had only a week to live.

Jeffery's story is a reminder that nothing is impossible for God and that the power of our faith will sustain us when the health we are claiming is not evident in the moment.

Choosing Life, Choosing Love

By Jeffrey Perry

I thought that I had somehow strained my back in the summer of 2000 when I started having back pain. Having gone through kidney dialysis and kidney transplant surgeries in the past 20 years, I was well acquainted with pain and discomfort. However, when this new condition became so intense that—in the middle of the night—I had difficulty breathing, I called my girlfriend, Catherine, and asked her to take me to the emergency room.

After being evaluated by a doctor, I was given a shot to relieve the pain and then sent home. The pain soon returned, worse than before. I was in and out of emergency four or five times when finally an X-ray revealed the cause of the pain: a liver tumor and non-Hodgkin's lymphoma. The doctor told Catherine that this was a catastrophic condition and I would need to be admitted to another hospital immediately.

I was rushed by ambulance to the nearby University of California-San Francisco Medical Center. As I was being wheeled into intensive care, Catherine grabbed my hand and said, "When we get out of this, do you want to get married?" I nodded *yes*.

I spent the next eight weeks in ICU undergoing chemotherapy and other treatments, but my condition worsened. Not responding well to chemotherapy, I lost 75 pounds during the first four weeks. In a kind of altered state of consciousness, I was somewhat aware but not able to communicate well with Catherine and family members.

My Choice

Even in this altered state, however, I did understand that I had an opportunity to participate in my own healing. If I didn't want to continue to be sick anymore, I could choose not to. One choice I made was not to have any more chemotherapy. It was doing a good job killing the cancer, but I felt that if I had any more chemo, it would also kill me.

Having been a health-care worker for several years, I had been with people who were making their transition. I knew one dialysis patient who consciously chose to stop dialysis and die. It took courage to make that choice, and I believed that I needed to respect this person and the path that he chose.

Upset with my choice not to continue chemotherapy, my family asked my friend Will to talk with me. He asked me if I wanted to live, and I said that I wasn't sure. I'd been through a lot and was extremely tired. His question was in relation to my choice to discontinue all treatment and go home, but it sparked my realization that I could also make the choice to live. There was so much more I wanted to do in life, and I wanted to be with Catherine. At that very moment, I chose to live. Even more than that, I knew that I would live without further chemo. I understood that it would take my body a while to catch up, but I knew that a healing had taken place.

After two months in the hospital, I was sent home to die peacefully. The doctor who discharged me believed that I had less than a week to live. Hospice was called in, and my family made funeral arrangements. Catherine, however, believed with me that I was going to get better. I was so weak and fragile that I could not eat or walk. My sister Jill, a nurse, came from Texas to help Catherine with my around-the-clock care.

Before I was hospitalized, I had been looking forward to my 20-year high school reunion. I had joined an e-mail group of classmates, touching base with people I hadn't seen in years. When those in the group learned I was sick, they e-mailed others. The prayer support grew daily. It was amazing. Church congregations as far away as Connecticut and Alabama were praying for me. A classmate I hadn't seen in 20 years wrote to tell me that she and her husband had just returned from Paris, where she had lit a candle for me in Notre Dame Cathedral. Rev. Richard Mantei and some members of Unity In Marin, where Catherine and I attended church, were in constant touch with us.

My friend William brought fresh flowers from his garden every day. Catherine created a healing environment in my room. She called Silent Unity for prayers and kept away any naysayers, because she didn't want me to be influenced by anything other than love.

Marry Me

My first night home from the hospital, I was only semi-coherent, and Catherine was sitting up with me. I could barely even speak, but I said to her, "Do you still want to get married?" "You remember that I asked you to marry me?" she asked. "I remember." Her answer was an enthusiastic "Yes!"

In the morning I called her parents. Catherine held the phone to my ear, and her mother held the phone to her father's ear. He had been diagnosed with cancer the year before and was nearing his time of transition. When I asked him for permission to marry Catherine, "Yes, absolutely!" was his reply.

The next day, I asked to talk with Rev. Mantei. My family thought I wanted to discuss my memorial service. They, along with Catherine, were gathered around my bed. Richard knelt down beside me and prayed. He then read the *Daily Word* message for that day. Afterward he asked, "Jeff, what is it I can do for you today?"

"Will you help us plan our wedding?" I asked, adding, "Catherine and I want to get married, but it would probably be a good idea if we wait until I get out of bed and start walking again." My health improved, and eight weeks later, Catherine and I were married.

The wedding took place on a beautiful, sunny day. Richard stopped part way through the ceremony and addressed our families and friends, saying, "Some thought we'd be here for a funeral about this time. Instead, we are here for a wedding and a celebration of life." It was a very touching moment.

I'm cancer-free now and active. I continue to live with kidney disease and have been back on dialysis for about four years now. I am currently awaiting another transplant. Dialysis is necessary, but I'm alive. Catherine and I are thankful that I am.

My health issues and challenges have been a catalyst for my spiritual growth and unfoldment. I remember the moment I chose to live and was healed. I knew that God was supporting me in whatever decision I chose. I knew at that point I could choose to die if I wanted to, and that would be okay because life is eternal. I understood that death, as we know it, isn't the end. It's the doorway to the next wonderful stage of life. I live each day with gratitude and in celebration of life.

Postscript

Jeffrey is the owner of an X-ray technology company in northern California, where he and his wife, Catherine, live with their two dogs and two cats. They enjoy traveling and are active in their church. Jeffrey is still waiting for a kidney transplant and remains cancer-free.

And more good news: Jeffrey and Catherine have adopted a baby girl. "Faith is quite another miracle in our lives," says Jeffery. "Catherine and I held a vision of adopting while working with different agencies, and then Spirit led us to the right people. Being parents to Faith is an opportunity of a lifetime. It all happened perfectly. We became close with the birth mom and were at the hospital for the delivery. The mother asked Catherine to spend the first night in the hospital with her and the baby, and then the next day we took Faith home."

5

LIFE

I love life—fully and completely!

My love for life is not dependent upon my circumstances. Whether I'm excited to be beginning a new adventure or content with everything as it is, I love life. Even when there is a concern about something or someone, I know that God is present, leading, supporting and carrying us through.

I am conscious of the order and balance throughout life—the obstacles and the opportunities, the extraordinary and the ordinary. I appreciate life and all expressions of it.

Being fully present in each moment, I am grounded in the presence of God within me. I experience joy in knowing that the activity of God is working on my behalf at all times. Making the most of each moment, I am enthusiastic about life, and I thank God for the experience of it all.

Keep your heart with all vigilance, for from it flow the springs of life.—Proverbs 4:23

Preview

In September 1999 author Fannie Flagg traveled from her home in California to Unity Village to be the keynote speaker at the annual Unity World Day of Prayer. I had the honor of introducing her at the *Daily Word* meeting on that day. Having done my research, I discovered an interesting fact: she had been runner-up in the Miss Alabama beauty pageant. As we waited for the meeting to start, I told Fannie that I was going to include this in my introduction of her.

After I introduced Fannie and she took the stage, one of the first things she said was that I said something that wasn't true. I slid down in my seat thinking, My gosh, what did I get wrong! Fannie went on to explain that she had never been in a beauty contest; her agent had created this "fact" as a publicity ploy. Everyone, including me, had a good laugh.

I'd forgotten that she was also a talented comedian and I felt honored to be the "straight man," setting the stage for all of us at Unity to experience this world-renowned author's sense of humor.

Works of Art, Signed by God

By Fannie Flagg

When I was younger, I was fascinated by the idea of miracles. I was always looking for one and searching for proof that they happen. I was so busy searching that I missed the real truth: every second of my life was and is a miracle! Even after I had accomplished everything in life that I thought would make me happy, I was still far from being happy. I was terrified because I had everything I thought I had wanted but I was still miserable. I knew something was missing.

What I didn't know is that most children of alcoholic parents don't feel secure because they've never been able to count on anyone or anything. Their whole lives revolve around the moods of the alcoholic parent. As a child, I focused totally on my father: Is he going to be drinking? If he's not drinking, is he going to be irritable or angry? And most of all, will he remember the promises he made to my mother and me when he was drinking and the promise he made while sober to never drink again? I never knew what was going to happen, and that's terrible for any child. With each broken promise, my trust crumbled a bit more till I finally shut down. I warned myself, "Don't trust in anyone, not even God, because you might be disappointed."

Alcohol abuse not only took my father away from me, it also took my mother, because all her attention was focused on him. So with both of us focused on him, we were cheated out of a normal mother-daughter relationship. I grew up a loner, afraid to care for anyone, terrified to trust in case my heart would be broken again as it had when I was a child.

The Search for Happiness

Upon leaving my hometown of Birmingham, Alabama, I moved to New York City and soon began working in television. I performed in theater, movies and the television show *Candid Camera*. I accomplished what I had set out to do: I had a lovely home, a wonderful career and friends who loved me—but I was not happy. I did not know how to love back or to give back. I began to have anxiety attacks, feeling nervous and full of fear. In 1980 I was starring in a Broadway musical. One evening as I was sitting at my dressing room table, I began to sob. I knew something was missing in my life, but I didn't have a clue as to what it was or where to find it.

A wonderful friend had sent me a gift subscription to *Daily Word*, but at first I merely threw it aside. Then one day I began to glance at it, and soon I was reading it every day. I thought of it as my fortune cookie or horoscope, and I thought, *Too bad this isn't true.* I secretly began to envy those who did have a belief in God.

Then suddenly, within a few months of being diagnosed with cancer, my mother died. She was young, only 58. I believe that stress weakened her immune system. She had so much stress as a child of an alcoholic and even more stress as the wife of one. My father put my mom, me and himself under a lot of stress. He died three months after Mom died.

During that time the only comfort I could feel came from reading *Daily Word*. I don't think I could have gotten through those times without it, for every day the message was just the one I needed. It seemed written just for me and somehow addressed what I needed to hear that day.

After losing both parents, I felt lost. I gave up acting and thought a lot about death and suicide. I was homesick for something, but I didn't know what. I had seen people who had complete faith, never questioned it, and I always longed to have that. I wondered: How did they get it? How were they able to just accept who they were and be happy and not question and all that? I went back home to Alabama looking for something, but I didn't know what. I began to drive around to all the old places where I had lived as a child. Then, on a cold, rainy November afternoon, I drove by the old family home.

The beautiful two-story white-frame house where my grandmother, her brothers and her sisters had been raised was now nothing but an empty shell, much as I felt I was. On that dark afternoon, with the headlights of my car shining on the windows of the house, for just a moment, I saw it the way it must have been years ago—all lit up and full of happy people. I stopped the car and cried for all the things that used to be. But out of that moment came the idea for a new novel, *Fried Green Tomatoes*.

Through Their Eyes

One of my characters, Mrs. Cleo Threadgoode, began to teach me about God. I saw God through her eyes. The more I wrote, the more each of my characters helped me begin to believe in God. My view of the world changed by seeing it through their eyes. They showed me nature, the beauty of simple things. They showed me how to love, how to be happy and appreciate things. They taught me about miracles—where to look for them and what they are.

I'm writing a new book, and the other day Aunt Elner, one of the characters, was telling a young man who said he had never had proof that God loved him to look at his own fingertips. She explained that God thought each one of us so special that He gave each and every one of us who ever lived, are living, and will live, a completely different and unique set of fingerprints—as a sign that we are special. She asked the young man, who was an artist, "Who else but the great Creator could create billions of different people and never repeat Himself?" The young artist was then able to see

God as an artist and realize that each one of us is a work of art, signed by God.

When I started my new book, I wondered where it would take place, and Missouri kept popping into my mind. I didn't know why, since I've never been there and don't know anyone there. And yet because my *Daily Word* comes from there and Unity started there, I thought that surely Missouri must be full of the sweetest people in the country.

Now, as I think back at how distrustful I was, I know that all the while, somewhere deep down, there was still that child who responded to what was true and what was pure. There was something so pure about Unity and the way *Daily Word* was written that I responded to it on a very deep level.

Daily Word was not out to do anything except help and comfort me. It didn't require that I do anything. It didn't demand anything of me. All it said to me was, "Look, I'm here as a friend if you need me." Soon I began to reach out to other children of alcoholics and felt relieved to find that I was not alone, that there were so many of us wanting to heal old wounds. Through my friends, I learned that the only way to truly heal was to forgive and turn everything over to God. And thanks to *Daily Word*, I had a better understanding of trust and believing in the positive.

For much of my life, I was scared and needed some sort of peace. It's taken a long time, and I'm still not great at it, but I'm making progress. All I have to do when I get stuck is look at my fingertips and remember I'm a work of art, signed by God.

Postscript

Fannie Flagg is a successful actress, novelist and screenwriter. Her books include the *New York Times* best-seller, *Fried Green Tomatoes at the Whistle Stop Café, Daisy Fay and the Miracle Man, Fannie Flagg's Original Whistle Stop Cafe Cookbook, Standing in the Rainbow,* and *A Redbird Christmas.*

Fannie received the prestigious Scripter Award and was nominated for both the Writers Guild of America and an Academy Award for her screenplay of the movie *Fried Green Tomatoes,* in which she had a cameo appearance. Any of us who are fortunate enough to catch TV reruns of *Match Game* are treated with Fannie's perfect timing of wit and comedy.

I'm always delighted when she mentions *Daily Word* in her novels. By the end of every book by Fannie Flagg, I have been blessed by stories of seemingly ordinary people who have shared extraordinary wisdom and love with me.

6

COURAGEOUS

I am a courageous and strong creation of God.

I may wonder, If life never offered challenges, how would I ever discover the depth of my courage and skills?

In truth, I have all that I need to meet any circumstance. I have the ability to respond to life's situations with poise, grace and wise action. And I do this in all matters by including prayer as my daily practice.

As I still my body and mind in quiet times of contemplation, I breathe gently and easily. I remember the truth about me: I am divine in nature. Whole in mind and body, I have all the spiritual faculties needed to triumph in any situation.

Taking a full, deep breath, I return my attention to my surroundings. I am a courageous and strong creation of God.

David said further to his son Solomon, "Be strong and of good courage, and act. Do not be afraid or dismayed; for the Lord God, my God, is with you."—1 Chronicles 28:20

Preview

Barbara Raven's poem "Badge of Courage" brought back memories of a lesson I learned years earlier. My husband and I bought 40 acres in the Ozark country of Missouri. As we scanned the green pasture and small forest of trees on our land, we knew we had picked the perfect site for our retirement home.

Two weeks later we returned to see that the floor of our forest was a carpet of black that continued halfway up the trunks of all the trees. There had been a runaway grass fire. Volunteer firefighters had been able to stop the flames, fed by high winds, before they reached our neighbor's house but not before they scorched our land and trees. The beauty of nature had turned into what looked like a scene of complete ruin.

That was an appearance, however, because the following spring new life emerged. Dried weeds and tangled undergrowth had given way to a carpet of green grass sprinkled with wild flowers. The trunks of the trees were still black, but a canopy of green leaves told the story of survival and life.

A Badge of Courage

By Barbara C. Raven

Before having elective surgery in July of 2001, I had a routine sonogram. That test revealed that something more serious was wrong. After further tests, it was confirmed that I had follicular lymphoma, a cancer of the lymphatic system.

I then began chemotherapy treatment. By the fall of that year, I was in excruciating pain. The chemotherapy had caused sores in my mouth and on my tongue. Pieces of my tongue literally came off. I couldn't eat regular food for five or six months.

Reading *Daily Word* and Unity teachings supported me during that time and continue to support me today. According to the doctors, this kind of cancer is a very tenacious disease that, when caught early, is managed through periodic chemotherapy.

My work as Rev. Paul Tenaglia's assistant in the office of the Unity Church of New York also blessed me at this time and led me to experience renewed hope from a most unusual source at a Unity retreat.

In July 2002, I attended our regular church retreat at the beautiful Trinity Conference Center in West Cornwall, Connecticut. I had made it through the worst time of my treatment. Because of the cancer, I still needed chemotherapy, but I was no longer in such a devastated condition. On the evening before the last day of the retreat, those in attendance observed a time of silence. We started right before dinner and didn't break the silence until the next morning after we had returned from what we called "our silent walk with God." After breakfast, we ended the silence, and those of us who chose to share talked about what we had experienced on the walk.

During my walk with God, I saw what I can only describe as a miracle tree: a huge tree with a deep gash that had been burned into its trunk by what I surmised was a searing lightning strike. I could almost feel the pain that tree must have suffered, but as I raised my eyes from that terrible scar to the rest of the tree, I was in awe of the truth that was revealed. There was a full canopy of healthy green leaves at the top of the tree!

Despite the appearance of the scarred trunk, this was a thriving tree, encompassing and healing its wound with new life and growth. This tree was a living metaphor for what I had been through. As I stood in front of the tree, it showed me a story of its own healing that literally took my breath away. Feeling both comforted and inspired, I took in a deep breath of air and walked over to a low stone wall on the property. Immediately I began to write words in my notebook that seemed to flow from my heart to my hand and out through my pen.

During our time of sharing messages that God had given us during our silent morning walk, I read "Badge of Courage," the poem I had just written. Later David Friedman, a Broadway composer who was helping with the music for the retreat, said, "Barbara, I was so moved by your poem I would like a copy of it so that I can set it to music." I was pleased by his request, gave him a copy of my poem, and heard nothing more about it for a while.

On the first anniversary of September 11, our church service was dedicated to courage and overcoming. The music director, Britt Hall, said to me, "I seem to recall that the poem you read at our retreat had something to do with the theme of this service. Would you be willing to read it this Sunday?"

"Of course," I answered.

That Sunday I read my poem.

> Tree standing so tall and proud
> Wearing her bold scar like a survival talisman
> A wound—a deep burnt gash in her trunk
> Reaching down to her roots
> Yet surrounded by the power of the trunk

Which somehow encompassed it
Allowing it to become one dignified whole
So that the scar is one with the tree—
a badge of courage.
It says, "Be not afraid—look how far I've come,
How tall I've grown; my leaves continue to unfurl
In the morning sun and the mist of twilight.
There is nothing to hold me back.
"No tragedy so great that I cannot overcome;
I have walked through the valley of the shadow
And returned triumphant to the Source of all.
My beloved sister, you can do—wait
You are doing the same, for we are one with God."
With that utterance no more needs to be said.

Afterward I took a seat in the front row. The next thing I knew, David announced that he had set my poem to music and began to play as Spiritus, the church's choral group, sang "Badge of Courage." Deeply moved, I began to cry.

Word about the poem grew. David read the poem to Patricia Neal, an award-winning actress, and she loved it. Patricia, who has recovered from three strokes, said, "This poem should be in every stroke center in the world," and she offered to record a reading of the poem.

Then David showed the poem to someone who was a cancer survivor, and she said, "The message of this poem should be in a book." Later a book was developed and published. In addition to that, Spiritus recorded "Badge of Courage" on their first CD.

I believe the real message of my poem is that no matter what we have to deal with in life, the power and the presence of God within will help us overcome it. In the darkest moments, we might feel that we are abandoned, but we never are. God is always present, and we experience this holy presence when we open ourselves to God.

I didn't always consciously know this during my treatment, but I knew it on some deeper level. At one point I asked a very spiritually aware person who had written a book about healing, "Tell me something. When you're in pain, how do you overcome it?" She said, "That's when I pray for other people."

That is a practice I began to apply in my life. If I woke in the middle of the night because my mouth was hurting, I would pray for those who might be suffering at that moment. The very act of praying for others relieved me of the intense pain and reminded me that we each have a badge of courage.

Postscript

Barbara Raven serves as director of pastoral care and as administrative assistant at Unity Church of New York. She trained with the prestigious HealthCare Chaplaincy, Inc. for three years in clinical pastoral education. Barbara has been a Unity Truth student for over 30 years and is dedicated to a life of service through ministry.

Barbara continues to have chemotherapy—twice a year—which she accepts as a gift that comes with a price. "There are times," she says, "when chemotherapy and the more recent diagnoses of congestive heart failure get me down, but I refuse to stay down. God is not testing me. It's just that life is made up of challenges. How I handle those challenges makes a difference."

7

UNITY

I am one in spirit with the family of God.

When I learn about people in other countries or become acquainted with people in my own community, I feel such joy over what we have in common.

While we may wear dissimilar styles of clothing, have diverse types of interests, or speak different languages, we share the common bond of being God's family. That bond unites us, allowing us to understand one another, share our joys and concerns, and feel compassion for one another.

Although I may not be close enough to offer physical comfort to others, I know that in Spirit we are united—heart and soul. And each day I reach out to hold my worldwide family in prayer, knowing that our oneness in God provides every one of us with all the comfort and support needed.

Finally, all of you, have unity of spirit, sympathy, love for one another, a tender heart, and a humble mind.—1 Peter 3:8

Preview

When Rev. Gregory Guice came to my office at Unity for a visit, he told me of his recent trip to Africa. I listened as he shared how the people of villages and cities of a continent far away had embraced the Unity teachings. Their story resonated at a deep level within me, and, having embraced these same teachings over 40 years ago, I felt a sacred connection with them.

Gregory is as much a man of this age as he is one who reveres the past and those who preceded him in carrying forward the Unity message. As he continued to tell me about his trip to Africa, I could see—in my mind's eye—the joy on the faces of those who welcomed him, the smiles of the children as they followed ahead on the road leading to their village.

Reading the next few pages, allow your imagination to accompany Gregory as he shares a most joyous and meaningful welcome home.

Welcome Home

By Rev. Gregory Guice

As an African American visiting Nigeria, I felt as if I were returning to my roots. As a Unity minister, I would be learning firsthand about the Unity movement in Nigeria. The movement that Charles and Myrtle Fillmore founded in Missouri in the 1890s had been introduced in Africa in the 1920s and had grown to more than 60 Unity churches.

I didn't know what to expect when I got off the plane in Lagos, Nigeria, a city of about 12 million people. Even though I didn't personally know anyone who lived in Lagos, I was welcomed like a long-lost brother by Unity minister Rev. Elizabeth Oyebode and a host of other Nigerians.

The next day, I boarded a plane for Port Harcourt. I spent the next week attending the Unity Harvest Retreat at a center in Rivers State of Nigeria.

Each morning about 50 of us in attendance awoke at 6 a.m. and jogged to a village about a mile away—singing and clapping our hands along the way. The sun rose as we entered the village each morning. After singing a few more songs, we jogged back to the retreat center and spent time in meditation.

At the conference, we joined in discussions related to Unity principles. We searched Scriptures and talked about their metaphysical meanings. One of the unique discussions centered on the challenges that Juju presented. Juju is a belief in magic associated with fetishes, charms or amulets. Many of the people of the villages were trying to make a transition from a Juju-based belief to a Christian-based belief. One woman at the conference asked us ministers: "What do I tell my brother who believes in Juju and was told by his Juju doctor that his children are evil? This doctor told my brother that unless he either separates from his children or buys jujus from him, my brother will be cursed!"

As Unity ministers, we shared our belief system. Knowing how entrenched that concept of Juju was in her village, we explained that we are each and every one a creation of God, and therefore, we are divine in nature. Because of the divinity of each person, no person has the power to place a curse on another.

The Juju doctor had placed the thought of the children being evil in her brother's mind, but her brother did not have to accept this error thought. I explained to her after the meeting: "God's presence is within your brother and his children. As they begin to realize that the divinity, power and presence of God are within them, they will collectively bring out the quality of God's greatness." We shared the "Prayer for Protection," affirming that only good would come to them.

As I traveled throughout Nigeria and visited several Unity churches, I discovered that despite the many challenges faced by the people I met, their faith and love for God and the Unity message carried them above their challenges. When these faith-filled people greeted me, I was aware only of their love.

One day as I was traveling in a car along a road full of potholes, several children ran to meet me. They walked in front of the slow moving car, playing trumpets and drums, escorting me to their village. The whole community was waiting outside the church. When I stepped out of the car, their cheers rang in the air. I felt the joy of being embraced with love and acceptance by my African brothers and sisters. Each man and woman shook my hand and thanked me for being there. They believed in the principles and the truth as expressed by Charles and Myrtle Fillmore. They valued the principles and teachings of the practical Christianity of Unity.

Chief Eze Onuoha Uma of Ohafia welcomed me. He and his ancestors had ruled that area for more than 300 years. This particular man, who was in his 90s, was educated in England. When the African civil war started, he left his job with Shell Oil to serve as a chief. During the war, he and his family had to hide in the bush to escape being killed. Unity ministers hid and fed him and his family during this perilous time. Later this man received a Nobel Peace Prize nomination. I was honored when he blessed me with the honorary title of a chief of love, peace and understanding.

Early one morning, I was awakened by a man who said, "Come, Reverend; follow me." This man led me to the center of a village in Ohafia to the home of Laeqaw O. Ezutah, the son of the man who founded Unity in that area. Laeqaw had built a kind of shrine inside his house, a library of Unity publications that had been collected from the 1930s to the present day.

We stepped out on the porch, and the children of the village gathered around as their mothers and fathers sat on the steps. Laeqaw, who was the head of this particular village, read the *Daily Word* message for the day, and then he interpreted the Scripture. Everyone there took time to pray, a daily ritual for them. How wonderful that these families wake up in the morning and say, "Let us read *Daily Word* together."

I will never forget sitting with the elders of the village that evening under a full moon as they shared stories and told me about the rights and rituals of their village. I asked one of the elders, "In your reflections of history, do you tell any stories of Africans who were taken into slavery?" He said, "Yes, we have kept these memories alive by telling them to our young people."

The next morning, we drove high into the hills, where Laeqaw pointed out the path on which slave traders took many Africans into slavery. Over the years, generations of villagers had kept that path clear as a reminder of the sons and daughters who had been lost to Africa. I understood why they welcomed me as a son who had returned home.

During my time in Africa, I learned the positive impact that Unity principles have had in Africa—principles of a God of love and of the sacredness of each and every person. I know this is a message of truth that is shared wherever people recognize the presence of God in all and as being expressed by all. This is a truth that is uniting the people of the world in faith and love.

Postscript

Rev. Gregory Guice is the minister of Unity of Lake Orion in Orion Township, Michigan. "I thank Rev. Lisa Davis and Helen Evwaraye," he says, "and the Building Bridges program at the Unity Church of Dayton, Ohio, who, along with Unity Christ Church, Fort Wayne, Indiana, funded and organized my tour to Nigeria."

He gives special thanks also to Silent Unity Church of Port Harcourt, Senior Revs. Dr. Amos Kalu and Okon Ebong, and Akin, Rev. Guice's guide and travel companion. "Sweet memories of those who welcomed me as a son returning home to Nigeria continue to bless me."

In 2007 Gregory Guice's 22-year-old daughter Morgan was killed by a drunk driver. Anger and punishment, not forgiveness, were on Gregory's mind as he traveled from Michigan to Florida to meet the young man who had violently cut short Morgan's life.

"When I came face to face with this young man, I saw someone who reminded me of myself when I was young. I, too, had done stupid things, but for the grace of God, they had not ended in such tragic circumstances." Instead of condemning the young man, Gregory forgave him and continues to correspond with him while he serves a sentence of eight to 12 years in prison.

This loving father and man of faith went on to say: "Morgan taught me so much about ministry in her short life, and by forgiving this young man, I am able to move forward in life and in my ministry."

8

DIVINE GRACE

I am transformed by the infinite grace of God.

In the tender moments of life, I have an opportunity to fully experience God's grace, and I gratefully give myself permission to do this. So whenever I feel vulnerable or feel that my life is out of control, I surrender any need to control and allow the grace of God to be my strength.

The scriptural promise that "power is made perfect in weakness" is a divinely true paradox. As I let the perfection of God express wisdom and strength through me, I am living this truth. Divine power is indeed perfect, and grace is revealed as I let go and let God.

The transformative power of God's grace is infinite. At one with God, I am strengthened with divine power.

"My grace is sufficient for you, for power is made perfect in weakness." So, I will boast all the more gladly of my weaknesses, so that the power of Christ may dwell in me.
—2 Corinthians 12:9

Preview

When I met Angela Williams at a Unity event on the West Coast, I felt an immediate connection with her. She talked about how the often necessary mobility of young families meant that many new parents didn't have a mother, grandmother or aunt living close by to help with the newborn. She smiled as she explained how much she enjoyed being a doula, helping young parents get off to a good start with the care of their babies.

As you will learn while reading her story, Angela has experienced both "up" and "down" times in life, but she has emerged fulfilled by being of help to those who need the love and comfort she was so willing to give them.

By the Grace of God

By Angela Williams

At age 19, I received a scholarship to nursing school, believing with all my heart that being a nurse was a wonderful way for me to express my spirituality. Taking care of God's creations, I would be serving God and letting my life be one that was dedicated to Jesus.

Early on in my training, however, I faced a challenge that I thought might cause me to leave nursing school. I could not tolerate the distinct aroma of patients who were very sick. I would often have to stop caring for patients when I smelled an odor caused by illness emanating from them. Sick to my stomach, I would run to the utility room.

One day while preparing to bathe a gravely ill man, I felt my stomach begin to churn violently, and I rushed to the utility room. I became still for a few moments, and my own healing began with this declaration: I am going back to this patient, and I will care for him as if I were taking care of Jesus. And I did, bathing the man from head to toe without any difficulty. I then changed his bedding and left him in a beautiful state of dignity and peace.

By the grace of God, I never again had a problem caring for a patient. No matter how dire the circumstance may seem, God's grace does flow through us when we are willing to put someone else's needs ahead of our own. Grace comes through us when we have compassion for others that surpasses our own comfort level.

Healing Love

During my early childhood while growing up in church, I had two dreams. One was to serve God by caring for others, and the other was to marry and have a family of my own. Following my dream, I married a doctor, and we had five children. Over the years, however, my dream became a nightmare. Being in a marriage that my spouse did not honor, I found my marital situation unbearable. A divorce, however, meant that I would have to leave the church that I loved so much. I knew that in order to preserve my self-respect and even my sanity, a divorce had to happen.

During this time, I found *Unity Magazine*. Reading it, I learned about God and the grace of God that was continually blessing all creation. Nurtured by an understanding that God accepted me as I was and loved me unconditionally, I felt a healing take place within me.

Several years after the divorce, still chasing the dream of a happy marriage, I married a second time. When I was diagnosed with cancer—just when I needed him most—my husband left me. I moved to California to be near my three daughters. I settled in San Mateo and began a new career by developing the first psychiatric home-care program for the county. Reaching out to care for others helped me to heal—this time from cancer. Many of my patients had AIDS and were in deep depression. The new program helped them cope with the disease and, when it was time, to die in a dignified manner. This work brought me into the hospice movement.

Over the years, I was the director of four hospice houses in San Francisco. Through the hospice staff, who were angels in disguise, I saw grace in action. Their loving care created a beautiful atmosphere for both patients and their families. People who were unfamiliar with hospice often asked me, "Isn't your work depressing?" My answer: "No, because I have found that even the slightest intervention in the lives of people who are feeling such desperation makes a difference—the difference between their feeling total despair and retaining their dignity." I have been at the deathbeds of hundreds of people in my work in hospice. I came to see the dying process as if it were the labor pains a person experiences before giving birth to new life.

Where God Leads Me

The grace of God was always there for me; however, when I pushed myself so hard by working 100 hours a week at the hospice facilities, I finally collapsed. Following my doctor's advice, I retired. After retirement, however, I found myself with a lot of extra energy and time on my hands. So I did volunteer work with a homeless shelter and started taking care of babies. I even wrote a book to help guide new parents in taking care of their babies during the first three months of life.

Some new mothers and fathers feel terrified and vulnerable about being parents. They may not have their own parents nearby to help out or not have had the opportunity to observe the parenting methods of their siblings. They need support to take on their new roles. As a certified doula, I go into homes to help care for the newborns for up to three months. Going wherever God has led me by circumstance, I have loved every situation. I have found throughout my life that I have to be involved in some kind of action toward caring for others, but I see that can be a bit of a deficit. At times, I am more like Martha, who went busily about her work, than like Mary, who sat at the feet of Jesus.

Yet all the while prayer and meditation have been a very important part of my life. Even a few moments in prayer can be a blessing. When I am not able to spend all day in prayer, I reach out for prayer support to people who are. I call Silent Unity for prayers for others or give people needing prayer support the Silent Unity prayer-line number. What a blessing it is to know that there is a place where people are communicating on a deep level with God 24 hours a day, 365 days of the year. I love Silent Unity, *Daily Word* and whatever helps people transcend the human picture of their difficulty at the moment. It's when we transcend the temporal that we live in eternity, knowing we are never alone.

Postscript

Angela Williams entered nursing school in 1953. She received undergraduate and master's degrees and completed postgraduate work. Certified as a Clinical Nurse Specialist in psychiatric and mental health nursing, Angela's service included work in veterans hospitals, cancer centers, psychiatric clinics and hospice programs. In 2006 Angela was honored as nurse of the year at her 50th class reunion. The alumnae association of her class of nurses awarded her for her work with the homeless and hospice population.

Angela's book on baby/infant care, *Angela's Baby Wisdom: Essential Checklists for New Parents,* is a compilation of 35 vital checklists distilled from the thousands of pages of information on prenatal infant care. Her book is laced with the wisdom of a registered nurse, mother of five, grandmother of 12, and a doula with eight years of experience helping mothers who have experienced postpartum depression. "My book," she says, "is dedicated to the Sisters of Saint Joseph of Rochester New York, whom I credit with teaching me how to love and serve."

9

MY FRIEND

Spirit unites us in a powerful bond of love and friendship.

I give thanks for you, dear friend. Whether we have walked the path of life together for a short period or for a long time, I believe we are participating in a divine plan of friendship. Being there for one another has helped us become more loving and compassionate people.

My life would not have been the same without you. Your love, your loyalty, your faith have enriched my life. Because of what you have shown me as my friend, I have become a better friend.

It's true that we have shared laughter, tears and understanding. Yet we have shared more than that from our humanness. Spirit within has been and will eternally be the source of the love that inspires us to be best friends.

Some friends play at friendship
but a true friend sticks closer than
one's nearest kin.
—Proverbs 18:24

Preview

The price *is* right that Bob Barker pays for being an animal-rights activist, for sometimes he does pay a price. This former host of the TV show *The Price Is Right* let his hair go gray because hair dye was tested on animals. He also quit as host of the Miss Universe pageant because contestants were given fur coats.

As an animal lover myself, I appreciate that Bob Barker is an advocate for pets and animals who cannot speak for themselves. (As I write this, Murphy—who as a puppy was rescued from hurricane Katrina and adopted by my husband and me—is sleeping peacefully at my feet.)

Thank God for You

By Bob Barker

Some of the most memorable and meaningful friendships in my life seemed to happen as if by chance. A chance meeting in high school with a girl named Dorothy Jo led to a wonderful partnership in marriage and in life.

Dorothy Jo and I considered another chance happening to be the most exciting moment for us professionally. Ralph Edwards had started a radio show called *Truth or Consequences* in 1940. Within the year, this program became the most popular radio show in the United States.

Later, Ralph started a television program called *This Is Your Life*. At about that same time, he sold *Truth or Consequences* to television. He could not host both programs, so he began auditioning in New York and Hollywood for a host for *Truth or Consequences*.

Driving his daughters to their ice-skating class one day, Ralph happened to turn on his car radio and heard me doing my local audience-participation show. He liked the way I worked and later called me. I did a series of auditions for him, and then, on December 21, 1956, at five minutes past noon, he called me and asked me to host *Truth or Consequences*.

Every year since then, at precisely noon on December 21, Ralph and I have met and celebrated our friendship and the wonderful day that brought us together.

What You See Is What You Get

I have never played a role on television, never been a detective or a cowboy or a doctor. I have always just been Bob Barker. And what you see is what you get.

When my wife was living, she often appeared on my shows with me. I have had my dogs and cats on the show, and I have talked about my personal life. The people who watch my shows regularly probably know me better than some of the people I know socially or professionally.

When Dorothy Jo passed, I lost my lifelong companion and best friend. I tried to stay as busy as possible in my work. I did a lot of shows at that time, and I accumulated a houseful of animals. Trying to keep my days full, I devoted more time to working for animal protection.

An Extraordinary Friend

And then one day, another chance meeting brought a dear friend into my life. A friend and I were driving along and saw a dog lying in the street. Stopping to see if the dog was injured, we discovered that it was dead.

Too late to be of any help to this dog, we turned our attention to a growling sound coming from the bushes at the side of the road. As we peered into the bushes, we saw this little dog—disheveled and obviously a stray. But what he was doing was extraordinary: he was protecting his friend's body.

We tried to coax the stray into my car, but he wouldn't budge. So we picked up the body of the dead dog and placed it on the backseat of my car. Immediately the little dog raced from the bushes, jumped into my car, and placed his head on his friend's body.

A Good Home

I told him, "You know, little fellow, anybody who's that filled with love and devotion deserves a good home, and you've got one!" And he has to this day. I gave him a name, Federico, and a place in my heart.

Just the other day, I lay down on the floor beside Federico and told him how much I love him. I said, "Federico, I thank God that I have you as my dear friend." And true to his loving nature, he wagged his tail and thumped the floor to let me know that he understood. I don't know where anyone could find a more devoted, loving friend.

I thank God for the dear friends and loved ones who have come into my life, dear ones like Dorothy Jo, Ralph and Federico. And even if it seems that they came to me by chance, I thank God for them and for the blessings they have been.

Postscript

Bob Barker was the host of *The Price Is Right* for 35 years and received 12 Emmys and the Carbon Mike Award of the Pioneer Broadcasters.

He established the DJ&T Foundation through his own resources to support low-cost or free spay/neuter clinics. The foundation is named in memory of his wife Dorothy Jo and his mother, Matilda (Tilly) Valandra.

Bob's work on behalf of animals has garnered him a long list of awards from prestigious humane organizations across the country. His autobiography is titled *Priceless Memories.*

10

IT'S POSSIBLE

All is possible through the power of Spirit.

If I am struggling to reach a goal, it might be because I am letting my own negative thinking loom over me like a mountain. My faith in God will move such mountains.

The spirit of God is the wind beneath the wings of my soul, giving me the encouragement I need to succeed. My thoughts are lifted above and beyond the physical realm to the higher plain of divinely inspired ideas. I am positive—a seeker of the better way.

And, at the very least, whenever I fall short of reaching a goal, I have gained experience and have an understanding of what could be a better way. What once seemed impossible is now made possible through my faith in God. I know that with God I can succeed. I can move mountains!

If you have faith the size of a mustard seed, you will say to this mountain, "Move from here to there," and it will move; and nothing will be impossible for you.—Matthew 17:20

Preview

When Rev. Joy Wyler and I served on a committee, brainstorming ideas for products and services that Unity could offer kids, I learned of her commitment to children. As she shared ideas, I understood that what she was offering would not only stimulate their minds but also enrich their souls.

I didn't know her personal story, however, until she submitted the story "Big Enough" for publication in *Daily Word*. Then I understood that responding to circumstances in her life from a place of love and faith was part of her preparation for being a minister who served children and people of all ages.

Big Enough

By Rev. Joy Wyler

When I was born in 1955 in a small hospital in southwest Missouri, the doctors and staff thought that a dwarf baby as tiny as I was had no chance for survival. They placed me in the back of the nursery and advised my parents not to hold me or become attached to me because I would not survive for long. On the third day, my 6-foot-2-inch father demanded to hold his little girl, reassuring the staff that his love was big enough to withstand whatever was to come. My parents took me home and I thrived. Ultimately, I reached my adult height of 3 feet 4 inches.

My father gave me two gifts that have lasted a lifetime. First, he loved me absolutely and unconditionally. My paternal grandmother wanted to take me to a faith healer, and my father forbade it. He said, "There is nothing to heal; my baby is already perfect." Second, he shared his concept of God, which was influenced by his Native-American roots and his study of other religions: God is everywhere present, within all people and places. Everyone is of equal value because all are children of God. God is in the rocks and mountains, lakes and oceans, animals, fish and birds. More important, God is a power and presence accessible to me.

During my childhood, I developed a very personal relationship with God. Prayer was half conversation and half intuitive, spiritual connection. I relied upon my relationship with God to get me through some rough times. Most of the adults in my life suffered addictions. My parents divorced when I was 7, and except for occasional phone calls and cards, I had little contact with my beloved father. He died when I was 12.

Making a Difference

Academics were my pleasure and refuge from a sometimes-chaotic home life. I wasn't big enough to ride a bike, but I never questioned whether or not I could do things. At age 5, I wrote a letter to newly elected President John F. Kennedy and received a reply. My picture was in the paper, and I learned I had a voice that could be heard. Graduating as salutatorian of my high school class, I decided to become a medical technologist and work in a hospital laboratory.

I experienced a bump in the road on my life's journey, however, when I applied for a job at a hospital in order to complete my degree. In an interview, I was first told that because I was not as tall as the laboratory counters, I was not big enough to be a medical technologist. Ultimately, I convinced a different hospital to take a chance on a student of short stature who had made consistently high grades in laboratory classes where the counters were quite high. I successfully completed that degree and later a law degree.

In the fall of 1984, I had just been sworn in as an attorney and had bought my own home. On October 11, I gave birth to a beautiful baby girl, Sarah Ashley. Much to everyone's surprise, I had carried her to term while working full time at the hospital and also finishing law school. Sarah was also affected by short stature but was otherwise healthy. Blissfully absorbed in my new role as a mother, I found it was more important to me than any professional career. On January 30, 1985, at the age of 4 months, Sarah died of sudden infant death syndrome, which was unrelated to her small stature. Losing Sarah seemed to tear a hole in my very soul. The whole center of my life dropped out. For the first time, I felt unable to connect with God.

In seeking a minister to perform Sarah's memorial service, my mother suggested I attend a Unity church. I did and found comfort and a recognition of some of my own spiritual ideas in the minister's message. I continued to attend the Unity church and began to take classes, including "Discover the Power Within You." Awakened to the concept of God as pure love, I understood that Sarah's life was a gift of love and I also discovered my own power to heal and change my life. The effect was profound.

Returning to the role of mother that Sarah had taught me to love, I adopted two dwarf children from India, first Victor and then Kari. As unique gifts from God who have offered me life lessons, my children have been a part of my spiritual growth.

We Are All Enough

Most of my academic and professional life has been spent challenging people to look beyond my appearance to see the strength of my character, the contributions of my capabilities, and the power of my faith. I may be half the size of others; however, I am not half the person. I have served as a medical technologist, a juvenile court and family lawyer, and legal counsel for a major children's hospital. In 2001 I left the practice of law to pursue my spiritual path more fully. In 2004 I was ordained as a Unity minister.

My life has long been my ministry. As I treat all people with love and respect, I am an example of someone who sees the Christ Presence in everyone. As I respond to prejudice or ridicule with determination and compassion, I help others to see that my power comes from my connection with God. As I pursue my dreams with confidence, I hope that others will be inspired to pursue their own dreams and know their own power.

Many people are judged by their appearance: their size, skin color or dress; their tattoos, piercings, hairstyles or other physical characteristics. My goal in ministry is to help everyone recognize that we are all enough because of the connection we have to a power greater than any challenge, greater than any belief in lack or limitation. Created in the image and likeness of that One Power, we are all big enough to create a life of abundance, joy, love and peace.

Postscript

An ordained Unity minister, Rev. Joy Wyler currently serves as the senior minister of Unity of Lehigh Valley in Emmaus,

Pennsylvania. Rev. Wyler also serves as adjunct faculty for Unity Institute.

Joy explains: "Writing the story 'Big Enough' was a prompting from Spirit, and it is a treat for me to hear how my story inspires others to see themselves differently." Her daughter is pursuing a career working with young children, and her son is living independently. Both are rising above their own challenges. With her own ministry continuing to unfold, Joy says, "I try not to underestimate the power of Spirit in each one of us."

11

MY VOICE

The words of my mouth and the meditation of my heart are true to Spirit within.

Although my voice is just one of many, it is powerful and effective, for I speak the truth of Spirit within me.

With my voice, I can support an existing condition or initiate change. I can speak in unity with others, or I can speak on my own with confidence.

Expressing my spiritual nature, I choose my words wisely, knowing that they are powerful vehicles for the fulfillment of the desires of my heart.

I honor myself and what I say, and I honor others for what they share. Through our united voices, we share the feelings of our hearts and the thoughts of our minds—each speaking from Spirit within.

Let the words of my mouth and the meditation of my heart be acceptable to you, O Lord. —Psalm 19:14

Preview

My son John's story was published in *Daily Word* a year after his chemo and radiation treatments had been completed. I attribute my years of being in the prayer atmosphere of Silent Unity, prayed up and positive, as the saving grace that kept me from collapsing in the family waiting room when the doctor told me that John had cancer of the larynx.

I immediately called Rev. Lynne Brown, the vice president of Silent Unity, for prayer support. Then Lynne and the rest of the staff of *Daily Word* formed a prayer circle; together they affirmed John's healing.

The night following John's diagnosis of cancer was the longest night of my life. I waited with John in his hospital room for the results of tests that would confirm whether the cancer had spread. I prayed through the night, as did John, our relatives and Silent Unity. My prayer was simple: "Thank You, God, that John is healed." This prayer of thanksgiving is one that I have spoken aloud or silently most every day for over a decade now.

A Grateful Voice

By John Bardwell

At the age of 35, I felt that my life was really coming together. I had just received a promotion at work, and I was happier than ever before in my personal life. I had quit smoking, gone on a diet, and lost more than 90 pounds. I was feeling really good—except for a sore throat that just wouldn't go away—even after I had taken some powerful antibiotics and allergy medication prescribed by my doctor.

After a few weeks with no improvement in my throat, my doctor referred me to an ear, nose and throat specialist. When he scoped my throat, he immediately saw what he thought was wrong. "Looks like a granuloma on your larynx." "What's a granuloma?" I asked. He went on to explain: "Well, it happens sometimes with people who have acid reflux. It's sort of a protective response to the acid attacking the larynx." Then he added, "We also see this in AIDS patients."

I knew in my heart that I did not have AIDS, but even a casual-sounding remark as that from a doctor made me anxious, and I had to deal with that anxiety.

I went in for outpatient surgery to remove the granuloma, but when I woke up after surgery, my life went spinning out of control: The doctor had cancelled the surgery after a biopsy showed the growth on my larynx was cancerous.

Because most people who have cancer of the larynx are much older than I was, the doctor wanted to be sure mine was not AIDS-related. A blood test was taken and a scan of my neck was done to discover if the cancer had spread.

I spent the longest night of my life in the hospital that night. I prayed, wanting to believe with every fiber of my being that the next morning I would receive good news about both tests. And thank God, I did receive great news. I didn't have AIDS, and the cancer had not spread to my lymph glands.

Saving My Voice

The ENT specialist recommended surgery to remove my larynx, but that meant I would lose my voice. I asked about an alternative treatment, which brought on a stream of specialists—an oncologist, a radiologist and a gastroenterologist. I felt as if I were watching a parade of doctors, with each one telling me what he or she thought was best for me.

I prayed about which would be the right treatment. My family, friends and Silent Unity, where my mom is editor of *Daily Word* magazine, were praying also.

The answer came to me: get rid of the cancer but try to save my voice. I chose to have a fairly new aggressive treatment—a combination of radiation and chemotherapy. I first had to have a feeding tube surgically inserted into my stomach, because the radiation would burn my throat, and by the end of my treatments, I would not be able to eat.

One night just before I started my treatments, I was thinking about what lay ahead and I could not sleep. So I got out of bed and logged on to the Internet to search for information about cancer.

I didn't find anything encouraging until I found the R.A. Bloch Cancer Foundation website. Years before, Richard Bloch had been diagnosed with incurable lung cancer. He was a tremendously successful businessman who had what most would consider the best doctors in the world. Yet he did not accept their diagnoses of impending death. He searched until he found a doctor who believed with him that he could beat cancer.

Richard Bloch did beat cancer, and late at night as I read what he had to say, I felt encouraged. He had a practical approach that I could understand: eat well, reserve your energy, think positively, have faith, and work harder than you have ever worked at anything in your life to beat this. Adopting this approach, I felt that I actually had some control over my situation.

Beating Cancer

I began a series of radiation and chemotherapy treatments that lasted four months. I used a visualization technique when I had radiation. Just before each burst of radiation was aimed at my throat, I would envision my healthy cells turning sideways, much like the slats on a mini-blind, exposing the cancer cells. There was a buzzing noise during those bursts of radiation, and I would envision cancer cells shrinking into nothingness.

I did have to work hard to get well. I was hospitalized several times—once for 10 days when a severe allergic reaction to a helper drug caused my blood pressure to drop drastically and my temperature to soar. My mom and a friend packed me in ice for two nights at the hospital to get my fever down. I felt as if I was going to die, but somehow I wasn't afraid. I just knew that this was what it felt like to die, and I was at peace. My blood pressure and temperature stabilized when the helper drug was eliminated from my treatment.

After my series of treatments was completed, I was unable to eat—except through a feeding tube—for four months. Scar tissue had formed a blockage in my throat. Five attempts were made to stretch the opening in my throat with tubes. I was hospitalized three times because my esophagus was torn during the procedure. I was beginning to wonder if I would ever be able to eat normally again.

Not once in all that time I was in the hospital did I have to spend a night alone. There were times I felt so bad I couldn't look out for my best interests, and having a family member or a friend there to look out for me was important.

I Did It!

And at times I just was not able to stay centered in my faith, but the faith of others upheld me. They believed for me what I was not able to believe on my own. God sent the right people to me and sent me to the right people. This was true when I was sent to yet another specialist who ordered a swallowing test—an X-ray taken as I tried to swallow some liquid.

I took a big swig of the liquid and tried to push it down. And lo and behold, some of it did go down. It hurt—more than anything I had experienced up to that point.

Later the specialists explained that a path was open in the throat. Because of the radiation, my throat had been slow to heal. And because I had not used the muscles in my throat that helped me swallow, they had grown weak. I had to relearn to swallow—teaching my atrophied muscles how to work again. The doctor looked me right in the eye, and I think right into my soul, and said, "John, I know you can do it!" He said it with such conviction that I believed him.

In a week I was able to eat a muffin. It took me 20 minutes to do it and it hurt, but as far as I was concerned, it was a great accomplishment. That was over a year ago, and I eat so well now that I have to be careful that I don't gain weight! And I continue to receive good reports each time I have a checkup.

I met Richard Bloch at Unity's World Day of Prayer in 2001. He was a speaker at the *Daily Word* meeting, and I thanked him for making a difference in my life. I'm sure he had been thanked by countless others, but telling him how much he had helped me meant a lot to me.

Having cancer, going through a divorce, or losing a loved one is a traumatic event. What I have gone through has caused me to appreciate my health, my family and the love of some wonderful people. On a very personal level, I have learned what is true of all of us: our bodies are miraculous creations that can heal, and our spirits are strong and eternal.

Postscript

John, who continues to be cancer-free for over a decade after his treatment, works as a business analyst for a large financial software company in Kansas City, Missouri.

He has a dog, Nona, who has a mind of her own when it comes to training. For instance, she stubbornly refuses to obey the "sit" command until he takes a treat out of the container. I guess this six-pound bundle of love and energy has to have proof before she delivers her part.

The following story is one in which I share how Nona came into John's life at just the right time. I believe she offered him love and encouragement in ways that were beyond what others or I could offer in words or acts of caring.

Nona, God's Special Creation

By Colleen Zuck

During the most difficult time of my son John's recovery from chemotherapy and radiation treatments, he became depressed. I tried to cheer him up. One time I showed up at his house dressed as Nurse Good Cheer with a bag of toys for my 35-year-old son. I had taped affirmations of healing all over me. I gave him a yo-yo, reminding him that life is like a yo-yo: when you're down, you give the little pull of a positive thought and lift yourself back up again. We ended up laughing and crying together.

Still wanting to do something to help him, I remembered that about a year before he was diagnosed with cancer, John had talked about wanting a papillon, a toy spaniel dog that has perky ears fringed with long hair. I started searching the newspaper ads for papillons. Telephoning several people who raised them, I was most impressed with one particular woman because she talked about the love and attention she gave her dogs. When she told me that she, too, was recovering from chemotherapy and radiation treatments, I felt this was more than a coincidence. It seemed to be a green light to ask John to go with me on a 120-mile round-trip to see about a puppy.

John seemed to perk up during the trip, and when one of the two puppies available was placed in his arms, his face lit up in a smile. As the tiny ball of fur rested on his chest, John and the woman talked about their experiences and their beliefs in a full recovery for both of them.

That tiny ball of fur came home with John, and I call Nona my "grandpuppy." She has offered John a lot of distraction because she is a high-energy dog, but she has given him so much more in the way of love. As John focused his attention on her, he thought less about his own discomfort.

John has healed, and Nona is a special creation of God's that has helped him in that healing. John has thanked me many times for Nona, and with all my heart, I thank God for John.

12

REJOICE

I rejoice in the fullness of life as a whole and holy creation of God.

During a challenging time, I may feel cut off from feeling any joy because of what is going on in my life and the lives of my loved ones. What I know to be true, however, is that there is a joy within me that can never be taken away from me by anything or anyone in the outer.

If ever an appearance of lack or limitation seems troubling, I know what to do. The joy that God has created within me is powerful enough, comprehensive enough, and expansive enough for me to experience a gladness of the soul whenever I call it forward.

As I do, I embrace the abundance inherent in every situation. I rejoice in the power of God to transform, heal and provide. I live the fullness of life that is possible because I am spirit, mind and body, a whole and holy creation of God.

You will have pain, but your pain will turn into joy.
—John 16:20

Preview

In 2008, when I met Esther Koch, my own mother had recently passed. Alzheimer's disease is often called "the long goodbye." This was what all of us who knew Mother as the "heart" of our family had experienced.

Her decline, at first, came slowly. Then over the next 12 years or so, it came in heart-breaking phases: her loss of short-term memory, lack of judgment about her own safety, failure to recognize family, diminishing ability to walk on her own and feed herself. There were, however, many moments of joy that we shared with Mother.

I know personally that the experiences and information in Esther's story will help you create moments of joy in the lives of your loved ones, whatever the circumstances may be. And I believe that the joy you give to others will return to you multiplied a hundredfold.

Esther was fulfilled in her career as a gerontologist and elder care advisor to many, but it was in her role as the tender, loving caregiver for her mother that she experienced her greatest joy and created lasting memories.

Creating Moments of Joy

By Esther Koch

My mother was a gracious, elegant lady, blessed by the grace of God and Unity principles that were the foundation of her belief that "God is working for my good."

Mother called herself a survivor, and survive she did—through numerous health challenges, finally succumbing to leukemia just days before her 88th birthday.

My father had passed away 20 years earlier, so during the last 10 years of her life, I was Mother's primary caregiver. I performed that role as an only child but with my professional expertise as a gerontologist and elder care advisor.

Caring for aging parents and being their advocate may be one of the most important and challenging roles that any of us may assume. Unfortunately, we can get so lost in all that we need to do for our parents that we neglect to truly be with them. We then miss out on what I call "moments of joy," some of the most beautiful and lasting times we will ever share with them.

Opening the Door to Gratitude

To get to moments of joy, we may need to get to forgiveness first. Mother and I both got to a place of forgiveness and never looked back. Although it was left unsaid, I know we both wished we had gotten there sooner.

Forgiveness opens the door to gratitude, and gratitude leads to joy. Yet, too often, sentiments of gratitude to a parent are left unexpressed or not expressed enough.

Some of my most cherished memories with my mother include reading Mother's Day cards to her—throughout the year. The last line of my favorite card was "My life is blessed because you are my mother." As I spoke these words to her, my heart overflowed with love, and I could see that her heart was uplifted.

Moments of joy are best expressed in the simplest of things. For instance, even when Mother was unable to walk, move in bed, or feed herself, she was elegantly dressed in a Hawaiian gown (Mother had been a professional hula dancer). Wearing makeup and having a flower in her hair, Mother had a twinkle in her eye. Dressing her this way brightened her day and the day of all who interacted with her.

Although cognitive ability might decline with age, one's capacity to feel does not. Even severe dementia is interspersed with moments of clarity. Knowing this, I never felt I could say "I love you" too often to Mother. My favorite response from her was "I know you do." She always said it with full clarity and emotion.

Daily Word, a Family Tradition

One of the foundations of Unity that provided daily moments of joy was *Daily Word*. My grandmother read *Daily Word* to my mother when she was a child, and my mother read it to me. We all requested the prayers of Silent Unity during troubled times and gave *Daily Word* subscriptions to many of our friends. *Daily Word* anchored our lives. Today, I have a link to its website on my home page.

During Mother's later years, I read *Daily Word* to her. Holding her hand and reading *Daily Word* to her was the highlight of my day. She never lost the ability to process and appreciate the daily message, frequently saying, "That was a good one."

Many days we thought the message was written just for us. When the message was for caregivers, I distributed copies to the staff aides. In her final hours, I kept rereading *Daily Word* passages and repeating the "Prayer for Protection." For me, it was the most loving, peaceful way to let her go.

Any Day Can Be Mother's Day

Creating moments of joy is a way to celebrate mothers on any day. If you need to start anew with your mother, don't miss the opportunity that Mother's Day brings.

Whether you are celebrating your mother in life or honoring her memory, moments of joy create blessed memories that last forever. And right in the midst of caring for a loved one, moments of joy are the best prescription for caregiver stress that I know.

And it is with deep appreciation and understanding that I offer the following blessing to the caregivers of the world:

Blessing for Caregivers

> May your life be without regrets.
> May you see the extraordinary in the ordinary.
> > And may someone be there to brighten your world as you age.

Creating moments of joy as you care for an aging parent:

> Focus on being with your parent, not just caring for your parent.
> Find joy in the moment. Be present to that moment.
> Know that joy is in the simplest of things.
> Seek to make the ordinary extraordinary.
> Forgive—a little forgiveness eliminates years of regret.
> Create in your parent's life the quality of life you want as you age.

Always remember that …

Denying your parent's aging will only lose you precious time. Start early.

Cognitive ability may decline with age, but the capacity to feel does not.

Postscript

Esther Koch is a gerontologist, elder care advisor and author. Her firm, Encore Management at *www.ENCOREmgmt.com*, provides educational and advisory services that assist individuals with issues associated with caring for an aging parent and their own aging. A sought-after speaker, her media interviews and articles have appeared on television, radio and in print. Esther is a 25-year member of Unity Palo Alto Community Church, in Palo Alto, California.

Esther expresses her gratitude in being able to share her story "Creating Moments of Joy" with the *Daily Word* and Unity communities, both locally and worldwide. She says, "Giving the Mother's Day sermon at my church that year, I was doubly blessed."

Since her story was published in *Daily Word*, she had a companion article published in *Unity Magazine*® and was interviewed on Unity.FM. Esther has received many e-mails, phone calls and letters from people sharing their elder care stories and how her story inspired them. The responses to her article came from the *Daily Word* family around the world—from as far away as Lagos, Nigeria.

13

FOUNDATION

I am building my life on the foundation of my faith in God.

A house is only as strong as the foundation on which it is built, so only the strongest materials and structurally sound plans are used in the construction of this important base.

I can also build a strong foundation for my life—a spiritual foundation that supports me with the strength to make it through any challenge. My faith with God is the foundation I create, one prayer at a time.

Prayer keeps me in touch with the spirit of God within—the spirit of life and love that nurtures and sustains me. This sacred relationship is the firm foundation for my other relationships.

My faith in God assures me that I will always receive the love and support I need. I am blessed with wisdom and strength.

Blessed are you, Simon son of Jonah! ... I tell you, you are Peter, and on this rock I will build my church.
—Matthew 16:17-18

Preview

Just as the issue of *Daily Word* with Robin Roberts' story was going to the printer, she made an announcement on *Good Morning America* that she would undergo treatment for breast cancer. Prayers for Robin started immediately in Silent Unity and everywhere in Unity Village.

Robin shared her journey of treatment and healing with the audience of *GMA*. There were days she could not co-anchor the program, but many more days that she did. As we watched and prayed, we witnessed not only Robin's healing, but also her faith, a gift that she gave to the world.

A Foundation of Faith

By Robin Roberts

I was incredibly blessed not to have to look outside my own home for my inspiration in life. Mom and Dad met at Howard University in Washington, D.C., and were the first in either of their families to attend college.

Mom put her career dreams on hold while she raised a family. Then she began her career in high gear. Among her high-profile endeavors, she chaired the Mississippi State Board of Education and served as president of the Mississippi Coast Coliseum Commission.

Dad was a member of the Tuskegee Airmen, America's first African-American military pilots. During his career in the Air Force, our family traveled all over the world and experienced many diverse cultures while stationed in other countries.

Mom and Dad always saw the good in everything and everyone, and they practiced this positive perspective while raising my brother, sisters and me. We were taught responsibility. When the streetlights came on, the Roberts kids went home. There was no "Oh, Mom, my watch stopped!" We ate dinner as a family by candlelight every night. We were in church every Sunday. We had a very strong spiritual foundation.

Mom and Dad believed that we could accomplish anything we set our minds to accomplish. Their positive message came across something like this: "Want to be a physicist on the weekend and split the atom Monday through Friday? Fine, you can do it!"

I Can Do It

I'm most grateful for growing up in a household like that and also for being encouraged to play sports as a young girl. I was fortunate to benefit from the wonderful Title IX legislation, which came along at a perfect time for me and other girls. It created opportunities and made college scholarships available to us.

My involvement in sports shaped me, and I always encourage those who are raising young girls to allow them to play sports. Because of the lessons I learned, I firmly believe I would have achieved a level of success in anything I had pursued, had it been education, medicine or sanitation. In sports I learned how to set goals and make sacrifices as a member of a team—all those things that, for generations before, boys had learned that had helped them go on to be successful men in life.

But most important, sports were just plain fun. I was fascinated by how fast I could run and how high I could jump. When it came time for me to choose a career, I chose sports broadcasting, a job in which I could focus on something I loved and felt passionate about. Although at that time there weren't many women role models in sports broadcasting, I believed I could do it. My parents had instilled in me the belief that whatever I wanted to achieve, I could. Today people ask me, "Robin, you've been a woman sportscaster at the highest level of ESPN and are now a co-anchor with Diane Sawyer on *Good Morning America*. What is the key to your success?" My answer is "being a child of Lawrence and Lucimarian Roberts. It's as simple as that." They were examples of faith and spirituality that became the very foundation of my life.

Spiritual Coat of Armor

My mother helped me when I moved from my parents' home in Mississippi to Nashville, Tennessee, for my first job away from home. When she saw that I had to get up very early in the morning and leave from a very dark apartment complex, she said, "Honey, I want you to say the 'Prayer for Protection' every morning before you open that door and go out into the world." My mom had first read this prayer in *Daily Word*, and I can't remember a time when this little magazine and the prayer were not a vital presence in our home.

Every morning since that time, no matter where I am in the world, I say this prayer before I walk out the door. It's my spiritual coat of armor. I wouldn't know how to begin my day without it. It's as essential to me as breathing.

Several years ago, we were filming a segment for *Good Morning America* showing how we began our day. A camera crew came very early to my apartment, and I went out to my balcony and did what I do each morning around 4 a.m. I said the "Prayer for Protection." Honestly, I never thought it would see the light of day. I expected to hear "It's not something we can show on national TV."

The response from the producers, however, was just the opposite. They liked it. They saw I was truly being me. I wasn't doing something to get attention or to make me look good.

I was being authentic. We went on the air with the segment and were flooded with requests for copies of the prayer. That was about five years ago; and since then, rarely a week goes by that someone doesn't ask me for a copy of the prayer.

The response to the *GMA* segment was beautiful, and I feel it really showed how people hunger for the Lord and for spiritual substance. I love it when somebody in the studio audience looks me in the eye and silently mouths the words "Bless you." I say "Bless you" right back. It's a way of uplifting one another, of communicating "I feel your spirit blessing me and I thank you."

A Life Built on Faith

We may all have feelings of being down at times, but we must never give up on ourselves or feel our situation is hopeless. My mother is an incredibly positive, spiritual woman. Yet when I called her recently, I could tell that she was down. Dad had passed away just over two years ago, and she was having a rough morning. She had read something in the paper about someone Dad had known and thought: *I've got to let Larry see this.* Her next thought brought her down: *Oh, that's right. He's no longer with me.*

It doesn't matter how strong we are. We all have down times in life. But when we hold on to hope and put ourselves in a position for good things to happen to us, we prepare ourselves for the good that's coming our way.

I believe in hope and prayer. And most important, I believe in strengthening my foundation of faith, because every day of my life is built upon that foundation.

Postscript

Robin Roberts' career in broadcast journalism spans more than 20 years. Present co-anchor of the ABC News program *Good Morning America* and formerly a contributor at ESPN, Robin has been repeatedly recognized for her journalistic excellence.

Following the devastation of Hurricane Katrina, Robin led the effort to rebuild her hometown of Pass Christian, Mississippi. Now an author, Robin's book is *From the Heart: Seven Rules to Live By*.

As co-anchor of *Good Morning America*, Robin chronicled her treatment and recovery from breast cancer on the show. One video was of her having her head shaved after her hair started falling out from chemotherapy. When Diane Sawyer asked Robin why she chose to share this scene with the *GMA* audience, Robin responded that her mama always said to "make your mess your message." Robin's message of healing is truly one of faith and hope for us all.

14

AFFIRMATIVE THINKING

Thought by thought, I affirm divine ideas.

What kind of thoughts am I allowing to take up residence in my mind? The answer is: thoughts that are life-affirming and, therefore, faith building. Such thoughts are a powerful way that I give direction and purpose to my life each day.

I realize that life-affirming thinking is even more powerful than positive thinking. Being a positive thinker, I believe that something good will happen and await its appearance. As an affirmative thinker, I give myself the go-ahead to claim the goodness of God that is already awaiting me.

Thought by thought, I am affirming divine ideas that are my God-given reality. Such thoughts are tools that give shape and form to my life.

O Lord, the God of Abraham, Isaac, and Israel, our ancestors, keep forever such purposes and thoughts in the hearts of your people, and direct their hearts toward you.—1 Chronicles 29:18

Preview

I didn't know what to expect in meeting Rev. Michael Beckwith. He had become what I considered a kind of "rock star" of spirituality after founding the Agape International Spiritual Center. This center, as described on the website for the church, is "a transdenominational spiritual community whose doors are open to all seekers in search of authentic spirituality, personal transformation and selfless service to humankind."

I had heard so much about Michael Beckwith the minister, who had helped thousands, millions, after his appearances on *The Oprah Winfrey Show* and *Larry King Live*, and the books he had authored and contributed to, including *The Secret*. I found him to be authentic to his message and enthusiastic about sharing it.

The first question I asked of him was this: "Tell me first about Michael Beckwith the man." Without hesitation, he began to share his story, one that surprised me and caused me to have an even greater appreciation of who he was and the blessing he was to all who hunger for a greater awareness of God.

Living in the Awareness of God

By Dr. Michael Bernard Beckwith

In my early 20s, I attended Morehouse College, primarily because Dr. Martin Luther King Jr. had graduated from there. Later I went on to the University of Southern California, becoming very involved in several groups that were protesting the war in Vietnam. One day while attending a meeting of such a group, I heard a voice within say, "If you took over the world tomorrow, would the world be any different, any better?"

I looked around the room at each individual and knew that because there was so much ego involvement, we could not succeed in changing the world. How could we help the world if we didn't first change ourselves? I left the meeting never to return. The very next week someone from that meeting shot another man over a power struggle.

I was still pretty wild at this time in my life—sharing marijuana with people and selling it to others, but I was about to experience a spiritual awakening. In a dream state, I saw my own death. When I awoke, I was aware that I was surrounded by the universal presence, which at that time I called "Love-Beauty." After this dream, I was determined to quit selling marijuana. However, there was a drug delivery in my home—the only time I had ever had drugs stored there. I planned to get rid of it, but before I could make an arrangement, I was arrested and taken to jail.

Listening to My Inner Voice

My inner voice told me not to worry because the life of drugs was over for me and I was going to be free. So all during the time that I was waiting for the court proceedings, I read books on meditation and spirituality, totally unconcerned about this world.

During my court appearance, the judge asked the arresting officer why he had raided my house. The officer testified that an informant had said that a dope deal was going down there. My attorney objected: "That's hearsay evidence."

The judge called a recess. Back in court three days later, the judge said, "Mr. Beckwith, I have learned there was no informant. I agree that the evidence was hearsay, so I have no other choice but to set you free. I hope I never see you in my courtroom again."

"You never will," I said and walked away.

As I returned home, the wind was blowing with great velocity. Standing outside my home, I looked up at the weather vane at the top of the house next door. I watched the arrow hold steady, pointing in the opposite direction from me. As I looked at the weather vane, I said, "God, if you are here, if what is happening to me is real, let the weather vane turn and point in my direction." I had barely gotten the words out of my mouth when the arrow spun around and pointed directly at me. I knew that the direction of my life had changed also. With tears streaming down my face, I surrendered my life to God.

Prayer and Meditation

That new direction led me to studying Eastern and Western mysticism. I developed a strong prayer and meditation practice that eventually led me to becoming a minister and founding my own spiritual community.

Through affirmative prayer, contemplation, meditation, study, fellowship and service, I became open to the thoughts of God thinking themselves through me. This was not simply a matter of positive thinking, because people can be positive that they are broke or positive that they are sick. I believe in affirmative thinking, affirmative realization. The very nature of the universe is affirmative, for life continues to affirm itself throughout eternity.

What most people call thinking is what I call the recycled conditioning of society. Authentic thinking comes from inspiration. The Japanese have a word for thinking, *kamkuru*, which means "to return to the realm of God." To me, God is the source of inspiration and therefore the cause of genuine thinking.

When we live an affirmative way of life, such as Unity teaches, we get in touch with our real nature, which is the life of God. The thoughts that begin to emerge from that contact are life-giving, beautifying and constructive. Our lives progress because we are progressive beings.

We're here on earth to continue to unfold, to reveal the infinite nature of the presence of God. We stay in a state of inspiration as we let thoughts from the Mind of God birth themselves through us. We become the instruments through which new ideas take shape, new ways of living emerge, and progress for ourselves and for the entire race takes place.

The joy in that progress, however, is not from our accomplishments themselves or the things we attain. Real joy comes from what we become as we are moving forward in our spiritual evolution. After a while, we realize our joy is really in becoming ourselves, in activating our potential. That's where our real joy, real happiness comes from.

Spontaneous Goodness

When one is saturated with a spiritual idea, something happens. I call it *spontaneous goodness*. We have insight and that insight moves us into right action. There's an action that's commensurate with our faith.

As human beings, we have a faculty of the presence of God in that we can think independently of circumstances, which allows us to be creative. Circumstances do not have the final word about our lives. As we think independently of circumstances, we begin to catch a vision that inspires us to describe our lives differently. The laws of the universe are there to support us in unfolding our vision.

We are not victims who have to live a life of fear, doubt and worry. There's a sacredness within all of us that reveals itself as we invite it to. With affirmative prayer and meditation, by studying and making a conscious contact with the presence of God, we experience a shift in attitude. And our attitude determines our character, our character determines our destiny—regardless of the past, regardless of present conditions.

As we consciously embrace the presence of God within our own souls and begin to affirm the absolute truth of our being, new thinking occurs that allows our new lives to unfold. This takes a little bit of work, a bit of attention. The result, however, is awesome, because we are then living in awareness of God and our own sacredness at all times and in all circumstances.

Postscript

Rev. Michael Bernard Beckwith is the founder and spiritual director of the Agape International Spiritual Center in Los Angeles.

He is the author of *Inspirations of the Heart*, *Forty Day Mind Fast Soul Feast*, *A Manifesto of Peace*, *Living From the Overflow* and *Spiritual Liberation*. He has been featured in the films *The Secret*, *Living Luminaries* and *Pass It On*, and on *The Oprah Winfrey Show* and *Larry King Live*.

As I taped an interview with Rev. Beckwith during lunch at the Unity Inn, I saw evidence that he is a man who lives what he preaches. I was feeling concern that the laughter from people nearby was interfering with me getting a clear audio taping of what he was saying. He must have seen some sign of frustration on my face. He smiled, closed his eyes, and said, "It's okay; let the laughter be." He was right. Later when I listened to the tape, the laughter in the background added to the power of his message.

15

IN THE STILLNESS

I enter into the stillness, a realm of infinite peace and tranquillity.

"Be still, and know that I am God!" At any time of my busy day I can reflect on this Bible verse and feel peaceful. As I become still, I know the presence of God.

I breathe and relax, feeling a sense of calm and quiet within me and surrounding me. I accept that I have completed each task to the best of my ability and used my time wisely and responsibly this day. I let this realization further relax and reassure me. Now separate from the busyness of the day, I am still and quiet. The calm is palpable.

In the stillness, I am in a realm of infinite peace and tranquillity. My senses are hushed, and I am aware of God. Peace prevails, and I have a heightened awareness of the healing presence that heals all. I am strengthened and fortified.

For God alone my soul waits in silence, for my hope is from him.—Psalm 62:5

Preview

Storytelling is an integral part of folk music, and Judy Collins' beautiful, pure voice opens all who listen to a portal through which we learn of the people and conditions from decades past.

My experience as I listen to her sing is one in which I feel the compassion, strength or faith that the story offers. She projects a beauty of sound that is palpable.

Listening to her sing "Amazing Grace" always bring tears to my eyes and gratitude to my heart.

My Prayer Place Within

By Judy Collins

My father sang and played the piano on his own radio show for 35 years, so I was raised with constant music in my life. When he started to teach me how to play the piano, I'm sure that my father never dreamed that I would someday have a career as a folk singer. By the age of 13, I was performing classical music in concerts.

But one day I heard a folk song called "Gypsy Rover" on the radio, and it changed my life. I started listening to and learning folk music, and when I was 16, I begged and pleaded until my father bought me a guitar.

The storytelling component of folk music spoke to my heart. Instead of playing alone at a piano, I began playing and singing in the company of other musicians who enjoyed the camaraderie of trading songs with one another and learning songs from one another. Being involved in the folk-music world, I felt as if I was part of a social circle of talented, friendly people.

My Spiritual Journey

I was strengthened by the spiritual quality of folk music. Although I grew up singing in the choirs at church, I was drawn to the message of a spiritual journey that most folk music addressed.

During my 41-year career as a folk singer, I have traveled on the road a lot, doing 60 to 80 shows a year, but I have loved every minute of it. There's nothing I like quite as much as being on an airplane or in the back seat of a car, traveling somewhere. I settle in with all my toys—my books, computer, tape recorder and CD player—and have a great time.

Keeping my spiritual connection intact is of great importance to me. One of the things that is so wonderful about *Daily Word* magazine is that I can carry it with me wherever I go and pull it out to read anytime. It's portable enough, and there is always something in the daily messages that pertains to me.

Sharing the Arts

I was asked to be a representative for the arts for UNICEF in 1994, and in that capacity, I have traveled to Russia, Japan, Bosnia Croatia and Vietnam. I lectured and wrote about UNICEF. They had been so much in the forefront of children's physical and emotional health. I became interested in an art therapy program they had started in Mozambique. The children there were growing up in such violent situations. Their villages were surrounded by land mines and were continually being shelled. I didn't realize how terrible their situation was until I actually went there on a visit.

I learned firsthand how helpful art programs were to these children. Doing something artistic such as singing, reading, playing an instrument or drawing helped them through some very traumatizing times. The arts are an important part of everyday life, but they take on even more importance when they help children and adults who are emotionally upset.

A Deeper Prayer Life

I was raised in a church environment, but folk music did so much in leading me into a deeper prayer life. I think prayer is the strongest antidote there is for negativity and fear. In my own work, I rarely start to write a song without first going to the prayer place within. It is essential for my own stability and emotional health to do that.

Like everybody else, I have gone through some difficult times. All the violence in the world—and the fear that even more will come—makes the journey of life difficult for people everywhere.

My own personal journey has included surviving the suicide of my son, and that's been extremely hard for me to do. Yet I don't think that we can really compare troubles and decide that one person's challenge is greater than another's.

We all have challenges, and we just need to know there are tools that help us overcome them. Prayer is a powerful tool by which we can maintain a strong connection with that greater force than ourselves, because alone we just could not handle it.

The truth that I feel strongest about is that, for all of us, our own inner guide knows what is going on and what is ours to do. It's an inside job and takes a lot of prayer, a lot of work, and a lot of trust, but that is when the real healing comes through.

Postscript

Judy Collins is an accomplished singer, songwriter, author, actress and filmmaker. Her career has spanned more than 40 years and includes a multitude of albums, top-10 hits, and gold and platinum status. Judy has founded her own record company, called Wildflower, and has devoted her time and talents to charity work for UNICEF and Amnesty International.

In 2001 she was honored with a lifetime achievement award from the National Museum of Women in the Arts. Judy's book, *Sanity and Grace: A Journey of Suicide, Survival and Strength*, focuses on the death of her only son and the healing that followed this tragedy. Judy wrote and performs "Wings of Angels," a ballad about the loss of her son. The song is currently available on *Judy Collins Wildflower Festival* CD and DVD, which includes guest artists.

I believe all who listen to Judy Collins will know in their hearts that they are hearing an angel sing.

16

STRENGTH OF SPIRIT

I have strength of Spirit, for the power of Spirit is within me.

Through various circumstances of life, I may be called upon to be physically, emotionally and mentally strong. At these very times, however, I might feel as if I'm not up to giving my best.

My best, though, does come about as I affirm that I was created with unlimited strength of Spirit. Focused upon the indwelling Spirit, I open my mind and body to currents of stamina and strength. My physical strength is renewed. I am able to remain calm in the face of disturbances. I have the confidence and the clear thinking needed to do my best, meeting my responsibilities and embracing opportunities.

I call on this inner strength of Spirit at any time and in any circumstance, for the power of Spirit is within me.

On the day I called, you answered me, you increased my strength of soul.—Psalm 138:3

Preview

Breaking news seems to travel so much faster now than it did in 1985 when terrorists held Jackie Pflug and other passengers hostage on a hijacked plane. Along with millions of others throughout the world, I waited and watched and prayed.

A decade later Jackie shared her story in *Daily Word*. Her story is one of extraordinary strength during a time of terror. It may be difficult for any of us to hear her describe what happened to her and some of the other passengers. Yet reading to the end of her story, we will allow our consciousness to rise above the terror and reach an understanding of what is true for us all: the strength of God that is within us at all times and in all circumstances.

Leaning on the Strength of God

By Jackie Nink Pflug

I was next, but I felt no fear—only overwhelming love as I began to picture in my mind the sweet, familiar faces of family and friends. One by one, I told them goodbye.

I had been returning to my teaching job in Cairo, Egypt, from a trip to Greece when the EgyptAir plane I was on was hijacked. The plane was now parked on the runway of an airport in Malta.

In the hours since the hijacking, several passengers had been killed by the terrorists because their demand for fuel to reach their destination was not being met. The two other Americans on the plane had been taken to the front, shot and dumped on the runway.

As I was led up the aisle of the plane, I silently prayed the Lord's Prayer.

A Vital Link

Prayer brought me such peace in this time of shock and chaos. As I walked up the aisle, I heard the murmur of prayers being said in different languages—Arabic, English, Hebrew. But no matter the language, prayer was the vital link for us in knowing the presence of God. I felt love and peace instead of hate and fear.

When I reached the door of the plane, there was an explosion in my head—a flash of light and colors, a tremendous bang, and a heaviness that spread throughout my body. I felt as if I was floating in air, but I was actually tumbling down the metal staircase onto the tarmac. I stayed conscious only long enough to realize something incredible: I was still alive!

I was one of the few passengers to live, for a few hours later, a rescue attempt was made and many of the passengers were killed. When the medics picked me up off the tarmac, they thought I was dead. But in the ambulance, headed toward the morgue, one of them turned me over, and I gasped for air. Immediately they changed our destination—from the morgue to the hospital.

Yes, I was alive, but I was also left with hearing, sight and memory impairments. In the next few years, I needed prayer and faith, friends, doctors and therapists to help me through to a healing.

I had been taught as a child to be strong and not to ask for help. So after the hijacking, I pushed myself to do the things I had once been able to do without much effort. I had taught special education classes, but after my head injury, I could not even remember that I was a teacher. I had nightmares about the hijacking, and I fought to hold back my emotions.

Healing From Within

When I gave myself permission to cry, to trust people, and to need people, I began to heal. A friend who had discovered her own spirituality began to teach me about mine. She encouraged me to listen to my own inner voice for guidance. Another friend called Silent Unity for prayer support and ordered me the large-print edition of *Daily Word*.

As I spent more and more time in prayer, in silence with God, I noticed a calm, comforting feeling growing within me.

I Had a Responsibility

I began to receive the answers to my prayers, and many times they came through other people. But most important, I realized that I had a responsibility for those answers. I didn't automatically wake up one morning and have inner peace; I had to work toward it. Maybe I couldn't take giant leaps, but I could take baby steps that moved me forward a bit each day in my healing.

I wanted to get back to a normal kind of life. I wanted to start reading beyond the third-grade level I seemed stuck with after the head injury. I wanted to be able to remember people and events.

In prayer, I asked for a way out of the deep depression that plagued me, and then, seemingly by chance, I was directed to a doctor and a therapist who worked with me until the depression went away. I have come a long way since then, but my healing is still going on.

As I gradually improved, people began to urge me to share my story. But I kept asking, "Why?" I didn't want to tell a story that was a message about suffering and pain.

God's Spirit Is Within!

I began to think about what I had learned from my experience and found that I had so many blessings: I had faced death without fear, and I found strength and faith I never dreamed I had. I also discovered that God's spirit is within me, that no matter what I go through, I can never be separated from the loving presence and power of God.

This is the reason I wrote my book: I could share a story of never giving up; of leaning on the strength of God within for guidance, for healing and for all the answers we all need. This is my story, but it is your story as well—in fact, it is everybody's story.

In my new role as a motivational speaker, I tell people what they already know intuitively is true: Blessings really do come from what appear to be challenges. I remind them to slow down and listen for inner guidance, to realize the importance of their priorities, to "not sweat the small stuff," to forgive and release their hurts, to check their values, and to make a very conscious decision about what they are doing, how they are spending their time, and with whom they are spending it.

I encourage them, and I encourage you right now, to pray, to talk to God as a friend. I encourage you to embrace the truth that is true for us all: When we honor our own spirituality, we discover the answers to our prayers and have the courage to claim them.

Postscript

On Thanksgiving weekend of 1985, Jackie Nink Pflug was a passenger on EgyptAir Flight 648, traveling from Athens, Greece, back to her teaching assignment in Cairo, Egypt, when terrorists hijacked the plane. Jackie was one of a few to survive the hijacking, but because of a serious gunshot injury to the head, she was left with physical challenges and memory loss. She captures the drama of her remarkable healing and spiritual awakening in her book *Miles to Go Before I Sleep*.

During the time I was editing this book, I saw Jackie interviewed on a TV program about survivors. That prompted me to contact her and learn what had been happening to her in the last few years. She had news to share. Doctors had told Jackie there were three things she could never do again: 1. Be employed. 2. Read above kindergarten level. 3. Drive a car.

Jackie has since become an author and motivational speaker, and she received a driver's license. Most important, she became a mother. Jackie has faced the challenge of cancer and is now cancer-free. In 2006 she traveled back to Malta to thank the people who saved her life. While there, she went to the very spot at the airport where the plane had been during the hijacking. "I sat down on the tarmac and said a prayer of thanksgiving for my life," she says. "We each have the choice to be happy or sad, to be stressed or patient, and it's important to choose wisely."

17

GENEROUS SPIRIT

The love of God inspires me to give generosity.

The love of God fills me with the spirit of generosity. Expressing this love from within, I am moved to freely share who I am and what I have. My heart and mind are open to those who are near and dear to me. I am generous with my love and kindness and with my gifts and talents.

In the same way, my loving thoughts and actions reach out to those who live on the other side of town, another part of the country, or another part of the world. God's love has been so freely given to me, and, in return, my gratitude infuses me with a spirit of generosity toward all.

God's love is reflected in the abundance of life's blessings. I honor this love by sharing God's unlimited good, giving to others freely and generously.

Each of you must give as you have made up your mind, not reluctantly or under compulsion, for God loves a cheerful giver.—2 Corinthians 9:7

Preview

As much as I admired superstar Denzel Washington, being a wife and mother myself, I wanted to interview his wife Pauletta. I had read and heard comments by Denzel in which he turned the praise being lavished on him as an actor and family man to give praise and credit to Pauletta.

Pauletta has a history of being an achiever: a child prodigy pianist, an accomplished actress, a devoted wife and mother. When I heard her story, however, I understood that more than all this, she is a woman of faith—a faith that is the foundation of all she is and does.

Giving the Gift of God

By Pauletta Washington

When I was about 16 years old, something very mysterious happened to me: I had a series of dreams over the course of a week in which I was in an elaborate, kingly court. Incredibly, I felt frightened and at peace at the same time. And as the dream continued night after night, it always picked up where it had stopped the night before.

In the final version, I was surrounded by beauty—beauty I could see and feel. I realized then that I was experiencing the kingdom of God. This was a spiritual awakening and a personal strengthening for me, for I realized that *I* was part of the kingdom of God and that whatever I did in life, I would do in dedication to God.

I was called a child prodigy because of my musical talents. From the age of 5 until my early 20s, I was in the entertainment limelight.

But even with all the extra attention I received, I was raised by the book—the book of Proverbs, which my father often quoted. And my mother was like the wise, gracious woman described in Proverbs—very much a wife and mother who unselfishly gave of herself for her family.

God Is Greater

When I finished graduate school, I left my home in North Carolina to be an entertainer in New York City. I felt as if I had been transplanted into another world. At one time I was so broke that I had no idea how I was going to survive. On my next visit home, I noticed a statement on my mother's desk: "God is greater than any problem that you might have." After reading this, I opened up to my mother and told her about my finances, but I also told her that my need was for more than finances: I needed guidance.

She gave me her copy of *Daily Word*, saying, "You need to read this and follow it. If you read it and believe it, then you will accept what it says is true for you." I did and I still do. So many times when I open *Daily Word* it applies to me.

I've called Silent Unity numerous times because of the power of this prayer ministry. Every time I've called, the person who prayed with me was so responsive and calm, so directed and focused. It is always just what I need. Being the wife of an entertainer and being in the limelight make it difficult sometimes to live the word, so Silent Unity provides a real foundation for me.

My husband, Denzel Washington, became acquainted with *Daily Word* during our dating years as I read it to him. He was an actor in the television series *St. Elsewhere* at the time, but we didn't know how long the series would last. So we had to be thrifty. I had planned our wedding but had no idea how we were going to pay for it. But, oh, how I prayed.

Creating a Sacred Space

I created a little altar for prayer in my apartment. On it I had my Bible, my *Daily Word* and a candle. This was a sacred space, and the power I felt while praying there was incredible. When the bills kept piling up, I put them on the altar and I prayed about them. For some reason, I left them there. Before I left New York for our wedding in North Carolina, I happened to look at the altar, and there were no bills there! As if by a miracle, they had all been taken care of.

People often ask us to what we attribute the success of our marriage and the great children we have. Well, it's no mystery—it's the grace of God and *Daily Word*, which is very much a part of the Washington family. Denzel and I and our four children all read it.

I have called to order *Daily Word* so many times because Denzel keeps giving them away! He carries them in his pocket. When he was doing the movie *Cry Freedom*, there was a dramatic scene in which his character was on trial. Portraying a real historical event, Denzel was calling on all his talent as an actor and reading down into the depth of human emotion, to the core of his spiritual strength, to portray a man being grilled unmercifully in a courtroom. Caught up in the drama of the story, Denzel kept touching his left side for some kind of assurance. What he was touching, inside a pocket of his suit, was a copy of *Daily Word*.

Denzel's father was a minister, and his mother was very active in the church as well. So the rich spiritual upbringing we both had has helped keep us together. It is as if we came to a table that was already prepared with dishes, napkins and forks; all we had to do was build on this. That doesn't mean it has always been easy, but we have remained faithful in believing that the greatest role in our lives is the role of being parents. We try to be examples of what we are teaching and saying to our children.

I'll always remember the time my father turned to me with tears in his eyes and told me that the greatest gift I had given him was teaching my children how to pray. (All four could say the Lord's Prayer by the time they were three.) He went on to say that the greatest gift in life is knowing God and knowing how to commune with God.

I believe it's this simple: To know God is to know love, to give to God is to give love, to be like God is to be God's love in action. Giving love is giving the gift of God, which is the greatest gift of all.

Postscript

Paulette Washington studied piano and graduated from Juilliard and received a master's degree in piano from North Texas State University. At age 11 Pauletta was the youngest person to belong to the National Guild of Piano Teachers.

She has starred in several plays on Broadway and has completed an international tour of her one-woman show. Pauletta and her husband, Denzel, are the proud parents of four children: John David, Katia and twins Olivia and Malcolm.

"I was blessed with parents who lived spiritually based lives every day," she says, "and I try always to be this kind of example for my own children." Reading *Daily Word* every morning and also giving it to others are traditions that her children are carrying on. John David has given his own copies of *Daily Word* to friends who were going through tough times. John David asked Pauletta to order a subscription to *Daily Word* for one of his friends, which resulted in his friend turning his life in a positive direction. Daughter Olivia keeps her copy of *Daily Word* in her car and reads it before she starts to school each morning. The Washingtons are truly a *Daily Word* family.

18

DIVINE IDEAS

I follow inner guidance in realizing my dreams.

Flashes of inspiration and spiritual insight sometimes come to me without introduction or invitation. It's as if divine ideas are floating in my mind and suddenly one drops into my awareness at the strangest moment—while I'm in the shower or driving, where no pen and paper are within reach.

Divine ideas also come to me in prayer and meditation as my heart receives a gentle nudge, an inner knowing. No matter how they appear, divine ideas stir me into action through revelations of truth.

As I follow inner guidance, I begin to envision new and insightful ways to manage the circumstances of my life. Divine ideas encourage me to dream a new dream and to move beyond current understanding so that I realize that dream.

Teach me your way, O Lord, and lead me on a level path.
—Psalm 27:1

Preview

As the granddaughter of Unity's founders, Rosemary Fillmore Rhea has always been a spiritual pioneer. She touched my life in a personal way when I was a teen: she was my introduction to Unity and *Daily Word*.

One morning I was watching a local children's show—not because it interested me (as a teen I would never admit that) but because there was little else offered on the few stations that were broadcasting at that time in our Kansas City area. The program that followed that children's program, however, pointed me in a direction that would eventually lead me to my 40 years of service at Unity Village.

The attractive, elegant female host of *The Daily Word* program seemed to be talking directly to me as she read the *Daily Word* message for the day. I don't remember what the word was, but I do remember her smile and her soothing voice, which seemed to flow from the speakers and wrap me in the assurance that I was a creation of God. I understood that *Daily Word* message came from Unity, but I was amazed, no, delighted, that only 35 years after women were given the vote, a woman was a representative of a worldwide movement.

Amazing to me still, about 20 years after I saw Rosemary on TV, something I hadn't dared to dream happened: I was working at Unity Village and would eventually become editor of *Daily Word* magazine.

The following is an excerpt from Rosemary's book, *That's Just How My Spirit Travels: A Memoir*. In this first chapter of her book,

Rosemary begins an engaging account of her life interwoven with personal memories of Unity's early days.

A Dream Come True

By Rosemary Fillmore Rhea

Once upon a time there was a place, an almost mythological place, situated in the very heart of America. It was there that I was born, and it was there that I spent my childhood. When I was growing up I had no idea how fortunate I was to live in such a place or what a remarkable family I was blessed to be a part of.

Unity Farm, as it was called at the time of my birth, was inhabited by a group of wonderful, imaginative souls who had a collective vision. In retrospect, I call it their magnificent obsession. They dreamed of building a city of God where people of all races, all cultures and all religions could experience their oneness in God.

The idea began with my grandparents, Charles and Myrtle Fillmore. One spring night, well over a hundred years ago, my grandmother—a frail, sick woman—walked into a lecture hall in Kansas City, Missouri, and came away with an idea that was to change her life. This idea was not to let go of her until she and my grandfather—who was soon set afire with it too—had founded a faith that eventually reached around the globe and blessed the lives of millions of people throughout the 20th century and now beyond.

In one hour, her whole outlook toward herself and her world changed. The simple, divine idea that she was the beloved child of God, that God's will for her could only be perfect life and wholeness, filled her mind and flowed through her body.

The old belief that she was an invalid, that she had been born frail and weak, that her time on Earth was limited, was washed away. Over and over she repeated to herself: I am a child of God, and therefore I do not inherit sickness. I am a child of God, and therefore I do not inherit sickness. In two years my grandmother was healed of the tuberculosis that was supposed to have taken her life. People learned of her healing and came to her for help, and they, too, found healing.

My grandfather had also been in physical pain most of his life due to a childhood skating accident that had left one of his legs withered and much shorter than the other. He saw what was happening to people who came to pray with his wife, but he had an inquiring, scientific mind and could not accept things on blind faith. He began searching for an answer to the amazing healings that were taking place in their living room. First, he read all the books he could find on religion and science. But the more he read, the more confused he became, as there were so many conflicting theories and theologies. So he finally decided if he was to find the Truth, he had to, as he described it, "go directly to headquarters—to God."

Night after night he would sit in silence, waiting for God to speak to him. He affirmed words of Truth, of life, and finally he made his breakthrough and his healing began. He wrote: "My chronic pains ceased. My hip healed and grew stronger, and my leg lengthened until in a few years I dispensed with the steel extension that I had worn since I was a child." So Charles joined with Myrtle and together they founded a school of what they called "Practical Christianity," and they named it Unity. They became magnificently obsessed with the idea that if they committed themselves to the Spirit of God within them, God would do the rest. They had

116

absolute faith that if they put God first, they would be healed, they would be prospered, they would be free.

They dreamed of a healing center that would reach around the world to inspire all people to move beyond their humanness into a conscious awareness of who they really are. This dream became a reality for them because they truly believed that "with God all things are possible." They had proved this with their own healing. Two sick, poverty-stricken people found a faith. They made the quantum leap from darkness and despair into the light of all possibilities.

Postscript

Rosemary Fillmore Rhea was on the cutting edge of broadcast journalism with *The Word*, which aired on more than a thousand radio and television stations and with documentaries such as *Around the World in Search of Faith*. Listed in *Who's Who of American Women*, she was actively involved with the International Relations Council and the White House Conference for Education for Missouri and now serves on the advisory committee for the Association for Global New Thought.

Rosemary remains a goodwill ambassador for Unity. She is in her office at Unity Village most days, participating in classes on the history of Unity and leading meditations during retreats. As both an ordained Unity minister and citizen of the world, Rosemary participates in activities and supports ideas that promote global peace.

For several months during the year, she lives in Montego Bay, Jamaica, where Rev. Pearl Davis founded Unity Kindergarten and Preparatory School. Along with hot lunches and classroom activities, Rev. Davis provides children with the truth about them-selves: they are special and important. And they can do anything they desire to do if they believe in it.

When Rosemary returns to Unity Village and on her travels everywhere, she shares stories about the children of the school. "They are one of the reasons I continue to go to Jamaica," she says. "I tell people that I meet, 'If you ever feel unloved, go visit the chil-dren at the school in Montego Bay. They are the epitome of love and welcome all with open arms.'"

19

ONE FAMILY

We are one family of God, rejoicing in sacred kinship.

We are united by birth or adoption, by marriage or inclusion. As friends we are family, and just as important—as family members we are friends. What really defines us is that we are all one family of God.

As we gather throughout the holidays and holy days in fellowship and celebration, in prayer and in communion, we bring the best to one another and we bring out the best in one another. Our best is being the love of God in expression.

We are caring and supportive no matter how far apart we may be. In our prayer times, we affirm the life, order, prosperity and peace that God has created us to have and to have abundantly. We are one family of God rejoicing in sacred kinship.

And the king will answer them, "Truly I tell you, just as you did it to one of the least of these who are members of my family, you did it to me."—Matthew 25:40

Preview

Some cartoons cause me to smile or laugh at the time but are mostly forgotten when I turn to the next page of a newspaper or magazine. Bil Keane's cartoons, however, are a kind of instant feel-good therapy that causes happy thoughts to linger in my mind. My favorite of "The Family Circus" is just one picture showing every footstep little Billy has taken on his way home from school. There was not one straight line taken during Billy's journey home. His footsteps show how he circled here and there because he found so many interesting things to investigate on his way.

This cartoon reminds me that even on routine days or on the same route I have taken hundreds of times there is new wonder for me to discover. I believe Bil Keane has a way of opening our eyes and hearts to the wonder of our relationships with one another and the wonder in all Creation.

The Happiest Place

By Bil Keane

As unlikely as it may seem when we are facing a problem, the challenge itself can turn out to be just what we needed to nudge us forward to receive our blessings. A challenge with allergies did just that for my wife Thel, our five children and me.

In 1958 each one of us was plagued by allergies. Working from nine to five as a staff artist, I was ready to quit that job in order to begin a career as a freelance cartoonist. I didn't know *where* I would be able to do that, but any location that was easier on our allergies would be fine.

During Christmas vacation, we left our familiar life in Pennsylvania and moved to a new life in Arizona. We moved knowing that blessings were in store for us, and they were! We not only found relief from our usual spring and fall sneezing bouts, but I was also able to work from my studio in our new home.

Being home full-time with Thel and our children—Gayle, Neal, Glen, Chris and Jeff—gave me daily inspiration for a new syndicated cartoon series "The Family Circus." It featured a mom, a dad and three children—Billy, Dolly and Jeffy. The syndicate agreed to distribute "The Family Circus" and sold it to 19 newspapers in 1960. Through the years, the cartoon has grown in popularity and is now featured in more than 1,500 newspapers. Readership is estimated to be around 100 million people daily.

In most of the mail I receive, people thank me for a particular feature that brings a touch of enlightenment to their day. And they thank me profusely for injecting a bit of spirituality into the cartoon. When I first started the cartoon, I was criticized for mentioning God or for having the children—in a playful way—mispronounce the Lord's Prayer. Jeffy would say, "Our Father, who art in heaven, how did you know my name?" Soon, however, people began to realize that the cartoon represented what was happening in real life—in their own families—and they loved it.

Later on, the characters of the grandfather and grandmother were introduced. In one cartoon, Granddad, who was a spirit in heaven, was sitting on a cloud enjoying watching his grandchildren down on earth. People wrote to say, "Thank you, thank you, for giving us a way to *show* our children where their grandfather has gone." The comic pages may have seemed an unlikely place for a portrayal of eternal life, but it was a graphic depiction that comforted both children and adults.

People relate to the spiritual insight of "The Family Circus" children when they describe heaven as a great big hug that lasts forever or explain that the snow-covered landscape is God's way of putting a topping on everything.

People also relate to "Mommy"—modeled after Thel, who was and is the backbone of our family. Thel has such a great grasp on family life and what it means to raise children in a loving, happy environment. I try to illustrate this philosophy in the cartoons, and I receive a lot of credit for it, but Thel is the real inspiration and heart of "The Family Circus."

I have heard that "Family Circus" cartoons are posted on refrigerators everywhere, and frankly, I would rather have my work hung on refrigerators, where it reaches many lives, than be secluded in a museum, where only a few can see it.

Our five children are all grown now and have careers and families of their own. We have eight grandchildren, and I follow them around just waiting for them to do something funny or cute! And the things our children did growing up seem even funnier now, so I incorporate a good bit of nostalgia into my cartoons, especially on the Sunday pages. I like to remind people of the joy of having children around the house, to encourage parents to enjoy their children at every age and every stage.

Since I began "The Family Circus" in 1960, the world and the family structure have changed dramatically. But the family unit is still important—no matter what the make-up of the family may be. I think this is the secret ingredient in "The Family Circus": the realization that a family setting in which the parents love their children and, in turn, the children love their parents is the happiest place in the world to be.

Postscript

Bil Keane draws the internationally syndicated cartoon "The Family Circus," which appears in 1,500 newspapers and is read by 100 million people daily. Bil became president of the National Cartoonist Society in 1981. He has won many awards, including the prestigious Reuben Award. Currently son Jeff is Bil's assistant in creating new cartoons. Nine grandchildren provide a whole new generation of inspiration for Bil.

When we were preparing to publish Bil's story in *Daily Word*, Elaine Meyer, assistant editor, corresponded with him on several occasions. She agreed to share something amazing that happened from getting to know Bil:

"Throughout our conversations, Bil said that, in addition to 'drawing' upon his own experiences for his cartoons, his family, friends and fans often send him their children's one-liners. We agreed that kids could inadvertently say the funniest things, and I shared with him something my daughter had said that had my husband and me practically rolling on the floor.

"Playing 'this little piggy' with her baby doll's toes, Caitlin, who was 5 at the time, was apparently struggling to remember the words to the rhyme. The original verse starts off:

> This little piggy went to market,
> This little piggy stayed home …
> Caitlin's version, however, came out as this:

This little piggy went to Walmart,

This little piggy went to Jones.

"Several months later, I was surprised to receive a package in the mail from Bil. Inside was a large, original "Family Circus" cartoon. In it Dolly is holding young PJ's toes, as she immortalizes Caitlin's words, 'This little piggy went to … went to … this little piggy went to Walmart …' Bil had autographed the cartoon "To Caitlin who said it first! Love, Bil Keane." Needless to say this cartoon holds a place of honor with our family and is displayed proudly and with great affection for our friend Bil."

20

FAITH

My faith sustains and uplifts me.

My faith acts as a silent prayer that never ceases. It is a vibrant understanding that forms the foundation of my life, growing stronger every day as I practice it. Faith is my inner knowing that the spirit of God is with me at all times, expressing divine qualities through me.

If a difficulty erupts with others, I am not intimidated by the appearance of disharmony or limitation. I act on a spiritual perception of what is true. I give expression to my faith in the power of God to create good out of all circumstances.

If I feel a dream is mine to claim, even if it may appear to be impractical, my faith enlivens my imagination to see the unlimited potential that is present. My faith sustains and uplifts me through all experiences in life.

But you, beloved, build yourselves up on your most holy faith;
pray in the Holy Spirit; keep yourselves in the love of God.
—Jude 1:20-21

Preview

At the beginning of my telephone interview with actress Betty White, two of her TV characters came to mind: the devious Sue Ann Nivens of *The Mary Tyler Moore Show* and the ditzy Rose Nylund of *The Golden Girls*. The reality, however, is that this diverse actress and avid animal rights activist is neither devious nor ditzy.

Throughout our phone conversation, Betty addressed me by name (Colleen) several times. Just before we ended our conversation, she called me "Carol," but I didn't correct her. A name didn't mean that much; I appreciated the warmth and friendliness this famous lady had lavished on me.

I don't believe a minute could have passed after we ended our conversation when my phone rang. Betty White was calling to apologize. The moment she had hung up the phone, she realized that she had called me by the wrong name. I thanked her but assured her that an apology was not needed. I sat there for a few moments after that call reflecting on how blessed I was to have spent time in conversation with such a gracious lady.

Faith Answered

By Betty White

My mother and I were really concerned—the small plane my dad was a passenger on was long overdue at the airport. We were scared to the point of feeling frantic. Suddenly I remembered a sign I had seen earlier that day in front of a church: "Fear knocked at the door. When Faith answered, no one was there." That message had caught my eye, and at the time, I said, "Oh, how charming."

But that faith message came back to me so strongly while we were waiting that I was able to be at peace about my dad. It was a message of hope that reached down inside me at a time when I needed it. Such a simple statement, but it says it all! It taught me not to fear the things that haven't happened yet and to handle things the best I can when they do happen.

As it turned out, Faith was right about my dad. The pilot found a hole in the clouds and managed to land the plane safely. But that message of faith stuck with me, and I've never missed a night of prayer since that time many years ago.

Although I've never been into formal religion, I've been on a very close conversational basis with God, my good Friend. And no matter what's going on, I can't go to sleep without a down-on-my-knees prayer. Every once in a while during the day, when something particularly good has worked out, I say a big "Thank You!" I don't ever ask for things or bargain with God. I ask for blessings. I believe in trying to do my best and then going on. If there's an extra mile to go, I try to go it.

I don't know how anyone can get through the day without being spiritually aware. But every once in a while, I have to remind myself to let go and let God, to not fight circumstances. I take a quiet moment, and that's where I get the comfort I need—from inside me. Sometimes I may tell myself, "Hold it! Cut!" and take a minute to just regroup. Then it's amazing how I get this surge of strength that comes from my quiet time with God.

A New Horizon

I was an only child, and my mother and dad were my best friends in the world. We adored one another, and we had such fun together. They supported me in being creative and getting into show business.

As a child, my ambition was to be a writer. I wrote the graduation play for grammar school, and, of course, I wrote myself into the lead as a princess. And suddenly, there on the stage, I thought, "This is nice!" In high school, I enrolled in a drama class, but World War II came along and show business got put on hold.

After the war, I started to audition for radio. I would have a line here and a line there, but there was a new media on the horizon—television. Casting directors began to say: "We don't have a radio job, but we have this television thing you can do. Of course, it doesn't pay much, but it's a wonderful showcase." Well, this wonderful showcase consisted of 14 or so television sets in the entire city at that time!

While working in television, I met Ernest Wilson, a Unity minister. The show was *Hollywood on Television*—a 5 1/2-hour *live* show. Whatever happened in front of the camera, you just handled it. Don Fedderson, who was the station manager at that time, brought in this great friend of his, Ernest Wilson, to give a positive thought for the day at the end of each show.

During our show, a woman would hold up the race results after each race at a nearby track. Our show was shown in half the bars in town so that the customers could see the race results. Ernest was thrilled about reaching out to such a new audience. He said: "I'm so delighted to come on right after the results of the ninth race. I'm in every bar in town! These people would never listen to me any other way!"

Unconditional, Uncritical Love!

Faith plays a big part in my work with animals—it's my main work! I'm into animal welfare and well-being. For 24 years, I've worked with the Morris Animal Foundation. We fund studies on the specific health problems of dogs, cats, horses and wildlife.

Pets so beautifully demonstrate unconditional, uncritical love. They take us as we are, for what's inside us. They don't worry about any of the external. It just seems so strange to me that people don't always give back in kind.

I recently lost my 16-year-old poodle, and I was devastated. My Timmy was a part of me, but I still have two other dogs. Cricket, 12 now, was a 5-week-old foundling when he came to me.

My beautiful little Shih Tzu, Panda, was in a cage for the first six months of her life, impounded as evidence in a cruelty case. I wasn't allowed to adopt her until the trial was over. When I did bring her home, I thought she would have been so traumatized by her experience that she would be this frightened little puppy. No way! She walked up to my two male dogs as if to say: "All right, boys. Here's how it's going to be from now on: I'm running this show!" And she does!

There are times I have to hang tighter and tighter to what I believe in without inflicting it on anybody else. Panda is a great reminder not to get discouraged about life in general. I hang on to my faith, to that arrow pointing to the positive as opposed to the arrow pointing to the negative—not only for my own salvation but also for the benefit of the people around me.

Sometimes it's hard to remain optimistic, but I can keep a positive spin on things. So whenever I find myself getting into a downward spiral, I turn around and start hiking faithfully back up the hill.

Postscript

Betty White's husband, Allen Ludden, would teasingly introduce her as "My wife, a pioneer in 'silent' television." Betty is, indeed, a pioneer in television, starring in such hit television series as *Life With Elizabeth*, *The Mary Tyler Moore Show*, *Golden Girls*, and *Maybe This Time*. Betty has received five Emmys and, in 1995, was inducted into the Television Academy Hall of Fame. She has authored several books, one of which is *Betty White's Pet Love: How Pets Take Care of Us*.

Betty appears to be busier than ever these days. She continues to have an active career: showing up as a celebrity contestant on TV game shows, a guest on early morning and late night talk shows, and a main character in movies. In 2010 a Facebook page was created to convince both Betty and TV's *Saturday Night Live* that she would be a "FANTASTIC choice to host SNL." A surge of Facebook subscribers offered their support, and, at age 88, Betty proved to be a hilarious host. In a 2010 Super Bowl commercial, she was also featured playing football with some 20-something men, which proved to be the most popular commercial of the program.

21

OVERCOMING

This is a wonder-filled day!

I may not recall the first steps I took as a child, yet I know from observing other children that such a challenge must have seemed great to me at the time I was learning. When my desire to move forward overcame any uncertainty and fear, I made great accomplishments.

The same power of God that was active within me then is enabling me to overcome challenges today. My overcoming is spiritually complete through God's power expressed in my thoughts, words and actions.

When I face a challenge at work or in my family or community, I know the power of God is working within me and through me to bring about an overcoming. Guided by God and filled with faith, I am whole and complete, inspired and fulfilled.

Immediately the girl got up and began to walk about (she was twelve years of age). At this they were overcome with amazement.—Mark 5:42

Preview

Actress Ann Jillian's story held special meaning for me, since my mother was also a breast-cancer survivor. When Mother was diagnosed, our whole family was devastated. The very word *cancer* can strike fear in the heart of the one receiving the diagnosis and also in the hearts of family and friends. Yet Mama was a shining example of faith and life for us all. Two weeks after her radical mastectomy, Mama prepared a delicious birthday dinner for me. For the rest of her life—more than 40 years—she lived cancer-free.

As a celebrity, Ann Jillian was able to inspire a great many people. By going public with her diagnosis of cancer and the treatment she received, Ann was an example to many of someone who not only survived cancer but has also thrived after cancer.

I believe you will be inspired by her story of faith and be delighted when you learn of a precious gift from God that she received seven years after she had gone through surgery.

Answering God's Call

By Ann Jillian

I had been attending the same church for years, yet I never noticed a quote by St. Francis de Sales on the side of the building until right after I was diagnosed with breast cancer, a time when I really needed this message: "The same Everlasting Father, who takes care of you today, will take care of you tomorrow and every day. He will either shield you from suffering, or give you unfailing strength to bear it. Be at peace then, and put aside all anxious thoughts and imaginations."

This was a message about faith—what my parents taught me long ago. It seemed that whenever I was with my mother and father, we could not pass a flower or look up at the clouds without one of them explaining the presence and creativity of God at work there. They found God in every day, in every way and instilled in me the wonder of what God did and could do. They taught me to recognize that life is precious and to always give thanks for the gift of life. They gave me a foundation on which to build my life, and the quote on the church wall reminded me that faith in God was within the very fiber of my being.

Surrendering to God

I have read articles in which conventional doctors recognized that prayer works miracles. Whatever faith they happened to be, whether they believed or not, they understood that faith does heal. We are all asked at times to validate what we believe, and cancer did this for me. It may have challenged my faith, but it also validated my faith. I knew that in order to get well, I needed to keep my eye on God, the Winner in all times and all challenges.

Surrendering is often equated with giving up. It never is when we hand over what we cannot handle to the One who can. Knowing that God loves us and cares for us is uplifting and healing. When the mind is at peace, the body then follows and is at peace and stress-free. And in that surrender to God, we may very likely be pointed in the right direction to receive help in our healing.

I surrendered and got well. God did it all—through me, through those in the medical profession, through the prayers of many, through the love surrounding me.

The Unexpected Gift

My husband Andy and I have been through much together. And like all marriages, ours is a work in progress. Every day, our relationship brings with it something new that we work on or enjoy or celebrate together.

We always knew we wanted children, but after 15 years of marriage it just had not happened. And we were resigned to the fact that it wasn't going to happen.

Seven years after I had surgery for breast cancer, Andy and I learned that I was going to have a baby. All children are blessings, but to have a child at my age, and after breast cancer, was an incredible blessing. My doctors were concerned about complications for me and for the baby, but as it turned out, none of their concerns came true. During pregnancy, I felt happier and healthier than ever. I laughed my way through my entire pregnancy. Andy Jr. weighed a bit more than nine pounds at birth!

Helping Others

When Andy Jr. was about 3 years old, my parents moved in with us—after a great deal of coaxing. Both of them had health problems and were quite elderly. Having three generations living under one roof was a revelation in many ways. Being the caregiver to my parents was a reversal of our roles; however, it was an answer to prayer. Andy Jr. got to know his grandparents, and they got to know him. In the remaining years of my parents' lives, Andy Jr. learned valuable lessons from them about love and family and helping others.

Since 1985 I have been on a mission to help others know there is life after cancer. We are all too familiar with the negative side of cancer, but there are legions of people who recover and go on to live healthy, happy, productive lives. I try to use the talents that God has given to me and apply them in ways that are entertaining and uplifting. When I perform, I sing and talk to my audiences. I share information such as the importance of early detection and treatment of cancer. I hope to both inform and entertain people.

We can all help one another—silently, through our thoughts and prayers; vocally, by what we say; and physically, by what we do. Random acts of kindness are a part of our mission in life, and when we embrace a mission to help one another, I truly believe we are saying "Yes, I am answering God's call."

Postscript

Ann Jillian is an award-winning actress, singer and motivational speaker. In 1988 she won the "Best Actress" Golden Globe award for her role in the television film *The Ann Jillian Story*. Ann writes a regular column for the website *www.thecolumnists.com*, and she displayed her three-octave vocal styles on songs composed by the late Steve Allen on her CD entitled *In the Middle of Love*. She is a recipient of the American Cancer Society's Award of Courage for her work to help others in the battle against cancer, and *Good Housekeeping* magazine voted her one of the most admired women in the world. She and her husband Andy maintain their own website: *www.annjillian.com*.

I recently went to *thecolumnists.com* and read some of the articles written by Ann. This is where she pays tribute to many of her entertainer friends. She also shares loving memories of her mother and father. Ann seems always willing to appreciate others, to hold then in the light of love. There must be thousands people who, like me, have never met Ann but have been blessed because she shared her life and faith.

22

IMAGINE

I imagine, accept and contribute to the highest and best possibilities.

Using my faculty of imagination, I explore possibilities, stimulate a flow of creative ideas, build on skills I have already developed, and discover new ones.

Having left behind any self-imposed or otherwise suggested limitations, I step into a world of opportunity and newness. Nothing seems routine or unimportant. Nothing is unattainable or impossible.

I view others and myself in the light of truth: We have unlimited potential to accomplish our hearts' desires. Launching out on my own or collaborating with others, I bring spiritual qualities of discernment and creativity to all my contributions.

I let my creative imagination act on whatever honors God and all that God has created. I imagine, accept and contribute to the highest and best possibilities.

But those who are noble plan noble things.—Isaiah 32:8

Preview

As adults, we may now tend to call the *heroes* of our childhood the *role models* that helped shape our lives. Most of us have had more than a bit of exposure to the cynicism in the world throughout our growing-up years. Then is it possible—as adults—for us to have heroes—people we look up to and admire and try to emulate?

I believe it is possible, and Bonnie St. John Deane is one of my heroes.

After doing a bit of research about Bonnie, I admired her for overcoming a physical disability to become an Olympic medalist. As she told me more of her story, however, I learned of her journey down a dark passage of life. As a young girl she had suffered abuse from an adult who was supposed to protect her.

Bonnie is living in the sunlight now and sharing how we all can emerge from the dark places in our past to live full and fulfilling lives. Thank you, Bonnie.

Yes, God, I Can!

By Bonnie St. John Deane

During my growing-up years, I lived my life in a mental landscape that I created for myself. In my imagination, I was a strong and graceful runner. I was beautiful and popular, and I could be anything that I wanted to be.

In reality, I had been born with a stunted right leg. My left leg was fully developed and continued to grow, but my right leg was extremely underdeveloped and short. I was unable to walk normally until I was 6 years old—when I had surgeries to stiffen my knee so that it wouldn't bend and to remove my right foot so that I could be fitted with an artificial leg.

Continuing to live in my imaginary world, I was able to control my thoughts and feelings while I was awake, but during the nights in the hospital, I would scream out in my sleep. A nurse would come to wake me from the nightmares so I could go back to sleep.

Much later in life, I understood what had caused the nightmares. It was only after my stepfather died when I was 18 that I allowed myself to remember he had molested me. Feeling so much emotional pain and trauma during my early years, I had stuffed the memories of abuse into the darkest corners of my mind.

Escaping the Pain

I escaped the pain through reading and through my active imagination. I read books at night after everybody else was asleep. I shut myself in the bathroom, turned on the light, and read on the floor. I read in the car and on the playground while other kids jumped rope and played kickball.

Then, when I was 8 years old, my mother gave me a brochure. On the cover was a silhouette of an amputee skier with the headline: "If I can do this, I can do anything!" I put the brochure away in a box where I kept a lock of my dog's hair and a rock from the Grand Canyon. I didn't realize it then, but the amputee pictured on the cover was showing me what I would someday be able to do.

In junior high school, I didn't feel popular or attractive. I wasn't good in sports, and I was always the last person picked when teams were chosen. The prayer chapel in the Episcopal school I attended became my sanctuary.

Living in the Real World

I was 15 when a friend invited me to go skiing with her and her family. She was kind and upbeat, never questioning that her one-legged friend could ski. This friend changed my life.

After that first ski trip, I resolved to step out of the mental landscape I was creating with my imagination and begin to live in the real world. I wanted to ski! When I first started, I lacked balance and strength, so I leaned over my heavy outrigger-style ski poles. I tried to race using regular poles, but I kept falling. Finally, I threw aside my ski poles, went to the "bunny," or beginners', hill, and began to ski without poles.

Learning how to ski with just one ski and no poles, I gained a tremendous amount of strength and balance. Then I was able to ski with poles, planting them in the snow so that I could pop up into the air and twist. This was a very exhilarating, free way to ski. In competition, I had to use outriggers, but I learned that they were not a crutch; they were an incredible tool that helped me go all the way to the Olympics and win.

The joy and passion I felt while training for the Olympics helped me discover my spiritual strengths too. At times, I had felt as if I was using prayer as a crutch. Then as I began to reach out more and more to God, I understood that while prayer is an incredible tool that had helped me heal, I had some work of my own to do. Just as I had had to learn to work with the outriggers instead of leaning on them, I had to learn to work with divine power instead of leaning on God.

Releasing the Past to God

I have a wonderful husband now and a precious daughter, but when she turned 4—the same age I was when I was molested—many painful memories came back to haunt me. There were times when I felt so down that all I could do was sit and cry. The love I felt from knowing the presence of God is the only thing that pulled me back up.

I could have let those destructive memories and emotions ruin my family and me, but I began to release them. I went to God in prayer, and God strengthened me so that I could heal.

I am making progress in my recovery, but I still have a way to go. The returning memories of the last couple of years have been more difficult than anything else I have ever had to face. Through turning to God, I am strong enough not only to face those memories but also to overcome them. And I know that because I can do that, I can do anything.

Postscript

At 16, Bonnie was a young girl with one leg and big dreams. Within five years, she became a Paralympics silver medalist, a Harvard honors graduate, and a Rhodes scholar. Bonnie has worked on Wall Street, in Europe and in Asia, and she has been an award-winning sales representative for IBM. A writer, speaker and president of SJD&Co., she also serves as a national spokesperson for Disabled Sports USA. Bonnie has been featured by *NBC Nightly News* as one of the five most inspiring women in the nation.

Bonnie has written and published several books: *Succeeding Sane, Getting Ahead at Work Without Leaving Your Family Behind, Money: Fall*

Down? Get Up!, and *How Strong Women Pray.* In her most recent book, *Live Your Joy*, Bonnie writes, "When you learn how to create joy in your life, you stop being a slave to what is happening in the world, and you become the master of your own destiny and emotions."

As an inspirational and motivational keynote speaker, Bonnie touches literally tens of thousands of lives each year with her messages of strength and courage. You can learn more about Bonnie on her website: *www.bonniestjohn.com.*

23

EXPECT GOOD

Divine energy is bringing about wonder in my life and in the world.

What are my expectations of this day, of any day? I expect the best and cooperate with its unfoldment.

I know that the spirit of God within me is greater than any challenge I could ever face. The life of God within me is a pattern of perfection that guides the activities of every cell and atom of my body. The wisdom of God is expressing as divine ideas that fill my mind. I act on them with gratitude and enthusiasm.

Every condition in life yields to the greatness of God that is in all and expressing through all. I expect the best from myself and others. I cooperate in loving, thoughtful ways with the divine energy that is bringing about wonder in my own life and the lives of those in my world.

Little children, you are from God, and have conquered them; for the one who is in you is greater than the one who is in the world.—1 John 4:4

Preview

Divine appointments between people happen in many different ways—all in divine order. As if by chance, two people meet for the first time and discover they share a faith, a belief that is the cornerstone of both their lives. This happened when Christine, one of my co-workers, met Brian Espy on a trip home from the West Coast. Brian had an assigned seat towards the back of the plane, and at the last minute, a seat became available closer to the front. The airline attendant seated him next to Christine. As Christine and Brian began to talk, they discovered their Unity connection. Christine served at Unity headquarters, and Brian was a member of Unity of the Heartland, a church just over the state line from Unity Village.

When Christine returned to work, she told me of this wonderful young man she had met on the plane and that *Daily Word* and Unity had changed his life. Christine encouraged me to ask him to share his story in *Daily Word*. I called Brian and he agreed to meet me at the Village. I will never forget the day I sat next to him and listened. I cried, as I do every time I read his story, but my tears cleansed my soul of any negative thoughts that had not been cleared away.

An Angel Named Terry

By Brian Espy

I have a great life now: a wonderful family, a wife and two kids, friends and a career. My life is great because an angel took me in when I was 15.

The first three months of my life were spent in an orphanage in Memphis, Tennessee. I was in foster care until I was adopted at age

5. In the 1970s, adoption screenings were less thorough than they are today, and a woman who was an alcoholic adopted me. I believe she adopted me and another boy in the hope that we would make her and her life better. That didn't happen. Continuing to drink, she became involved in one abusive relationship after another.

We moved often and survived on welfare and the charity of others. Mom took us to many different churches—for handouts. When the people in a church caught on to what she was doing, they cut us off. Mom would be very angry and talk about the self-righteous church people. She taught me that religion was a bad thing. At a very young age, however, I listened to that still small voice within me and innately knew right from wrong.

Every evening when I was young, I would read a verse from a Bible I had received from one of the churches I had attended. I didn't understand much of what I was reading, but I thought that if I read the Bible and prayed, God would forgive us for the bad things we were doing.

My Turbulent Adolescence

When I was in sixth grade, living in Michigan, I ran away from home for the first time. I took my Bible with me but was picked up by the police and taken back home. Mom became increasingly more abusive toward me—both verbally and physically. I thought God had abandoned me. At age 11, I started drinking to numb myself to the turmoil that swirled around me.

By the time I was a freshman in high school, I drank daily. The father of one of my friends convinced Mom to put me in a juvenile drug and alcohol program. This was at the local treatment center where, believe it or not, Mom was a drug-and-alcohol abuse counselor for adults.

Spending time with the other teens and the counselors of that program, I felt I belonged to a family for the first time in my life. At the end of my 30 days there, Mom decided to move us to Albuquerque, New Mexico. Once there, she became involved in another abusive relationship. When that man kicked her out of the house, she told my brother and me that we were on our own.

I was 14 years old at that time and spent the next year living on the streets of Albuquerque. Still attending school, I did odd jobs, mostly garden work, and I drank every day. Around the holidays, I would look in the windows of the houses I passed. Catching glimpses of families inside, I cried out: "God, why can't I have a family? That's all I want!"

The Road Ahead

Just to get by, I sold drugs and items I had stolen. Sitting underneath a pine tree in a park one evening, I suddenly knew where the road ahead would lead me if I didn't stop drinking. I had noticed that a 12-step meeting was being held in a building I passed as I walked from the park to school. "Okay, God," I said, "here's the deal: I'm going to give this program one shot. If it doesn't work, I'll go ahead and drink myself to death."

My clothes were dirty, and I had long stringy hair. I was an angry teen who was afraid of people, so when I attended the meetings, I sat quietly, never saying a word. After a couple of weeks, one of the men said, "If you'll open up and talk a bit, we'll take you to eat." I liked that deal. I was really hungry.

At each meeting, I opened up a bit more to the group. One member offered me his spare bed. I had a place to sleep. They helped me with my homework, and I started doing well in school. Several of the men went before a judge, asking if they could officially adopt me. Instead, the judge located my mother and sent me back to live with her.

One of my friends in the 12-step program drove me to meet Mom. I begged him, "Please let me stay with you guys!" "Remember the things that we've taught you over the last three months," he said. "You're going to be okay." He had to literally pull me out of his car and put me into Mom's van. We were on our way to Wichita, Kansas.

I ran away so many times in Wichita that I was labeled a habitual offender, placed in juvenile jail several times, and finally sent to a boys' home. I didn't drink, because I felt that God was living up to our deal. I attended a 12-step program in Wichita, and there I met my guardian angel—Terry, a former Marine Corps drill sergeant and recovering alcoholic.

My Life Turned Around

Terry took me in, saying, "If you live with me, you have to make your bed and go to school every day. You also have to have a job. I'll take care of everything else." He threw a copy of *Daily Word* across the table. "I want you to read this every day. Then you'll have a *Daily Word* assignment." If the message for the day was on living in the present moment, I wrote one page about how I had lived in the present moment that day. Then Terry and I would talk about what I had written.

In short order, Mom had me picked up by the police, and I was sent to jail. Terry brought me my *Daily Word*, explaining, "Your assignments don't stop while you're in jail. We're going to do this by the book."

Finally Mom gave up, and Social and Rehabilitation Services told Terry, "He's yours—nobody else seems to want him." While living with Terry, I graduated from high school with honors and went on to college.

No matter how difficult my younger years were, I believed that God never let me down. I had Terry, and later, a wife, son and daughter. I became a successful executive, flying all over the world on business.

A few years ago, Terry was hospitalized with throat cancer. Even when away on business, I would fly back home to visit Terry every Thursday evening. Continuing our *Daily Word* lessons, we sat and talked until he couldn't talk anymore. If I came to visit him upset about something, he would point to the *Daily Word* on his bedside table and say, "All that matters is this." Then he would point to my head and say: "Your world is between your own two ears. Everything that you create, you create in your head. You have a choice whether you want it to be good or bad. But remember, the universe is always trying to bring you good."

When Terry's condition grew worse, he was put on a breathing machine. When he was ready to go, he was taken off the machine, and there was a window of time, about three minutes, when he could talk to me. I was holding his hand, and he said, "I'm so proud of you." He looked at a picture of my daughter and son, and a tear ran down his cheek. Then he spoke his last words to me, repeating them several times: "You are my son. You are my son."

I could have given up at any time during my early life, but that still small voice, the spirit of God within, spoke to me.

Then Terry came along to be my angel. He still directs me to this day by what he taught me as a teen. I learned from him to get out of the way and let the universe bring me good.

Postscript

Brian is the owner of a sales consulting company, MobileForce Communications. He recently co-founded another company, PufferFish (*www.PufferFishNow.com*), which helps small companies reduce their telecommunications expenses while enhancing their online presence.

He reports that the Espy family continues to do well and offered the following examples of how they enjoy life even more when they spend time together: "After I finished an adventure race in the mountains, my family met me for a week of camping, whitewater rafting, fishing and hiking. We had a blast and even had a bear in our camp!

"I am now the head coach of my son Chase's Little League baseball team, and we are having a great time. Being involved as a parent with a child in youth sports has brought up some painful memories from my past. As a young person, I loved sports (especially baseball), but I never had anyone to work with me or show up to my games. Eventually, the other kids got the support they needed, and I was left out of the sports scene because I couldn't afford to continue financially, emotionally or physically.

"Working with Chase, however, is healing me from my own past and offering me powerful life lessons for living in the moment."

24

OPEN AND RECEPTIVE

I am open and receptive to the blessings of God.

With a willingness of mind and heart, I am aware of and receptive to the activity of the spirit of God.

Blessed with the gift of life, I know that every breath I take is an affirmation of the life of God being expressed as me. I am blessed by the abundance all around me—nutritious food to eat, a place to call home, clothing that keeps me comfortable.

I welcome people into my circle of loving family and friends, for we are here to give comfort and support to one another.

All blessings originate with God. I appreciate the blessings I have and I am open to new ones as they come into my life. I embrace new ideas that help me grow. My loving heart inspires me to give thanks for the infinite abundance of God.

Everyone who asks receives, and everyone who searches finds, and for everyone who knocks, the door will be opened.
—Matthew 7:8

Preview

We have all probably heard the timeless adage "A friend in need is a friend indeed." When a friend is in need, we can answer the call to be a helping hand, giving the gifts of our finances, attention and time. Unity minister Carl Osier, however, was the recipient of a gift that was beyond what money or time could provide.

I had the privilege of knowing both Carl and his friend Rev. Jim Rosemergy. Along with many others, I prayed, as a precious gift of life was given and received in love and with thanksgiving by these two men.

In this chapter, we will learn Carl's story—in his own words. The next chapter will be in the words of Jim, the giver of the gift. Both stories are deeply personal but devoid of ego and attention. Both men are testimonies to the spirit of God expressed as love and faith.

Gift of Life

By Rev. Carl Osier, M.D.

The last five years of my career as a physician were spent caring for patients in hospice. Prior to this, I had considered myself an agnostic. In hospice, I witnessed the positive impact of a relationship with a loving God on people who had only a few weeks left to live.

I saw their faith in God become more and more of a focal point of their lives. Of course, they grieved the loss of life, but it was the peaceful way they were facing death and dealing with loss of function that inspired me.

Belief in a loving God made a difference for their families too, because they knew their loved ones were eternally enfolded in

God's love. These relatives were saddened by what their loved ones were going through, but their faith in a loving God sustained them. It allowed them to say good-bye, releasing them to the ever-present love of God.

My Spiritual Journey

My observations in hospice prompted me to begin the quest of my spiritual journey. I started with a meditation group and then began a class on metaphysics. Toward the end of the 12-week class, I found myself asking, All right, what am I going to do now? I looked in the community newspaper and saw an ad for a Unity church. I attended once, twice and kept going. Unity had such an impact on me that, after a great deal of prayer, I chose to leave the practice of medicine and become a Unity minister.

Several years later, I was able to apply the life-affirming principles I had learned in Unity in a deeply personal way. I was in the process of doing some financial planning. As a requirement for an insurance policy, I had a routine physical exam. The exam showed protein in my urine that should not have been there. Further tests by my family doctor revealed a continuing deterioration in my kidney function. I began seeing a nephrologist (kidney doctor) and had a kidney biopsy. I was diagnosed with an illness called IgA nephropathy.

With this condition, IgA protein lodges in the kidney, forming blockages. At this time, there is no medical cure for this chronic illness. It may progress slowly over a period of many years or lead to end-stage renal disease, requiring dialysis or a kidney transplant. I had hoped the disease would stop or stay steady for me, but it progressed over the next few years.

Living From Faith

I learned that living from a faith in a loving God made it possible to face what was happening to me with very little fear and without dwelling on the question "Why me?" I felt at peace. I was aware of the gifts that were coming to me through this experience that I had not consciously asked for. For instance, I understood that life—even at its most challenging times—is a gift. I felt ready for whatever happened, even when my kidney function drifted downward and I was surgically prepared to begin dialysis.

That's when Joann, a minister and colleague at the Association of Unity Churches International, approached me about e-mailing Unity ministers in the field, asking for their prayer support and if anyone would be willing to be a kidney donor. It took me a little while to say *yes* to Joann sending this e-mail, but I did.

The Generosity of Others

By the end of the first week, 11 willing donors had responded to Joann's e-mail. I think this speaks volumes about the generosity and courage of my friends and colleagues. Rev. Jim Rosemergy was the first to be tested. Jim was a match in blood type and one antigen marker. These days there can be a transplant even if no markers match, but Jim and I had a match, allowing me to take fewer medications and avoid many possible complications. Jim went through a whole series of tests, which confirmed that he was in excellent general health and had excellent kidney function. Every test was a green light.

The fact that the e-mail went out May 27 and my transplant was able to be scheduled for June 23 knocked the socks off the transplant team. Jim arrived the day before surgery, and we prayed together in my office. We met again and prayed together the morning of our surgeries. Back at the Association, my co-workers held a prayer vigil through the day. My new kidney began to work as soon as it was "stitched in" (as the surgeon likes to say).

Prayer Support

I believe that prayer made all the difference—before, during and after the surgery. Jim's ongoing prayer was: "I love Carl; my kidney loves Carl." My prayer affirmation was: "I'm preparing a sacred place to receive and nurture Jim's kidney."

Since the surgery, I require only an eighth of the usual dose of immunosuppressant medications. Now when I climb stairs or just walk down the hall, I don't have to pause and catch my breath. I have my energy back!

I learned a lot about prayer during this journey. Prior to this, I had understood the phrase "lifted up in prayer" to be a figure of speech. Now I know that to be lifted up in prayer is a physical experience.

I learned to reach out to people, anticipating their generosity and support. This is important for anyone who is going through any kind of challenge. If there are times when fear does creep in, we find relief in letting the prayers of the people around us, of the Silent Unity prayer ministry, and of our church family support us.

Gift of Life

I'm trying to take care of this tremendous gift that life is. I am aware that God gave me a life extension through the kidney transplant. I'm aware that the story I have shared with you is about so much more than Jim or myself. It's about the gift of life. It's about the generosity of people and about prayer making a positive difference. It's about allowing oneself to ask for and expect support. It's about faith in a loving God and being thankful to God.

I do thank God every day, several times a day, for the gift of life. And each time I think of Jim, which I do every day, I give thanks for his generosity. And as Jim and I both say, "Everything looks just a little different now."

Postscript

Ordained in 1993, Carl was the first minister of Unity Fellowship Church in Norwalk, Connecticut. He currently serves as vice president of Minister and Ministry Services Association of Unity Churches International.

June 23, 2010, marked the sixth anniversary of the gift of normal life for Carl made possible through Jim Rosemergy's tremendous act of generosity and the skills and care of the transplant team of St. Luke's Hospital in Kansas City. Jim and Carl are both healthy. Carl reports: "I have not had any rejection episodes, I have normal kidney function, and I continue to take much lower than average doses of anti-rejection medications. The words that came to Jim in his dream say it all: 'Only love makes this possible.'"

Over the years, about 20 families who are *Daily Word* readers have contacted Carl. Some called because they were preparing for transplant. Some called to celebrate a transplant that had just happened. But they always said that the *Daily Word* story about Jim and Carl blessed them, inspired them and gave them hope.

25

GIVING

I give, and I am greatly blessed in return.

I may have received help from friends, family or even strangers at a time I needed assistance. I give thanks that they have been there for me and for others.

I, too, am open to giving to those who need help in everyday and unusual circumstances. Whether someone needs a ride to the doctor, a sitter for a child or a meal at the end of a pay period, my inner guidance reveals what and how I am to give.

The wondrous, miraculous gift from this experience is that I cannot give without receiving in turn—much more than I have given. As I acknowledge and appreciate the dedication of others to be of service, I myself am encouraged to give. I offer what I have of my time, talents and skills.

Give liberally and be ungrudging when you do so, for on this account the Lord your God will bless you in all your work and in all that you undertake.
—Deuteronomy 15:10

Preview

When I began to serve at Unity in January of 1969, Lowell Fillmore, son of the founders of Unity, was still coming into his office. More than that, Lowell would walk around to say hello to employees, and sometimes, to our delight, tell us a corny joke. My office in Publishing was small and had no windows. When Lowell arrived at my door, however, he filled that room with light. I was a beginner at Unity, but Lowell made me feel special and that what I contributed was important.

More than 20 years later, Jim Rosemergy, a vice president of Unity, would also visit employees. He didn't tell the corny jokes I had loved to hear from Lowell, but, like Lowell, he made me feel special and that what I was contributing was important. Each time Jim came by, he was a reminder that the warmth and caring of the leaders of Unity was a tradition that continued, and I'm happy to say it still does.

When I learned what Jim was giving to his friend Carl, I wasn't surprised. I knew that Jim was being true to the caring person he is. If ever you met Jim, I'm sure you would agree.

Love Makes This All Possible

By Rev. Jim Rosemergy

In the early 1970s, after flying 100 combat missions in Vietnam, I resigned my commission as a naval officer and entered the Unity ministerial school. I graduated in 1976 and began my ministry pioneering a church in Raleigh, North Carolina.

Over the years, I served in several other churches and as an executive vice president of Unity. In 2001, my wife Nancy and I answered the call to found a new church in the Missouri Ozarks.

One day in May 2004, Nancy and I were checking our e-mail messages. As we read an e-mail from Joann, a colleague who serves at the Association of Unity Churches International, we turned to each other and both said, "Yes, I'll give a kidney to Carl!"

Joann had asked for the prayer support of ministers in the field and also for volunteers to be a kidney donor for Rev. Carl Osier. Nancy and I said *yes* to being both donors and prayer partners. Carl's blood type was A-positive, and Nancy's blood type eliminated her as a donor. According to my dog tags, my blood type was 0-positive, qualifying me as a universal blood donor.

Incredible Joy

Being the closest to Kansas City, Missouri, where the transplant would take place, I was the first donor to be tested. I took blood and urine tests. About this time a state of joy and euphoria started to rise within me. Nancy questioned me, "Do you know you're acting as if you're going to a party?" I said, "Yes, but I can't help it." It was a serious matter, but I felt an incredible joy just thinking about being able to give.

A few days later, we were lying down to take a nap, and I said to Nancy, just kind of kidding, "Wouldn't it be something if my blood type changed to match Carl's?" About two minutes later, the phone rang. The nurse said: "I have some good news. The urine test is okay, and the blood tests are fine. I want you to know, however, that you don't have type 0 blood." My blood type was actually the same as

Carl's. Even better, we also had one antigen that matched, which improved the possibility of a successful transplant.

Two days of extensive physical tests were scheduled: CAT scans, X-rays and more blood tests as well as a psychological exam. It was a power-packed couple of days. Because Carl's kidney was failing, he had been prepared for dialysis with a shunt implant—dialysis was imminent. The plan was to try to see if everything could take place before Carl had to begin dialysis. And within a month, I was in one hospital donating a kidney and Carl was in another hospital ready to receive that kidney, never having to be treated with dialysis.

My surgery was laparoscopic, which meant less scarring and an easier recovery than if I had had a more traditional surgical technique. The first person I saw when I came out from under the anesthetic was a welcome sight: a former employee of the Silent Unity prayer ministry whom I had known while serving at Unity. He was now the head nurse of the operating room. The first thing I asked was, "How is Carl doing?" As soon as I was told Carl was doing well, I drifted back to sleep.

The next thing I remember is waking up in the ICU and realizing that Nancy was holding my hand. The following day, I was taken in an ambulance to the hospital where Carl was and given a room right across the hall from his. A bit later we were able to visit. Everybody took good care of us. I was released in 48 hours.

Life-Affirming Words

Carl and I will always have a special bond. We have each made a full recovery and believe this has to do with the inner work that each of us did. I took Myrtle Fillmore's approach of understanding that the life and intelligence within the cells of the body respond to life-affirming words. I was telling my kidney that it was going to find a new home with a wonderful man who had lots in life to give. From the beginning my affirmation was: *I love Carl, and my kidney loves Carl.* That was before I understood that it was really Carl's kidney; I had only been carrying it all those years! Carl used his own affirmation: *I'm preparing a sacred place to receive and nurture Jim's kidney.*

Through Eyes of Love

The second night after my surgery, I had a dream: Staring at my hands, which were a white translucent blue, I could see through them. My whole body became translucent. Hovering horizontally about two feet above the ground, I moved into a vortex of light and then popped through into a world of vibrant colors. This was a world of colors such as I'd never seen before. I heard a voice: "Love makes this all possible." I understood that I was seeing everything through the eyes of love.

I received an incredible gift—a glimpse of the real world and a yearning for the way life can be and is intended to be. From a spiritual standpoint, my understanding of this dream has quickened and deepened my yearning to live a life of love and to know, without a doubt, the joy of giving.

We tend to think of a need as something that is lacking or not present, but it really isn't. Through love we become sensitive to needs and recognize that they are actually gifts that are presented to us on a daily basis. If we accept these gifts, then we will experience the joy that Jesus talked about when he said: "Until now you have not asked for anything in my name. Ask and you will receive, so that your joy may be complete" (Jn. 16:24).

Full joy comes as we recognize a need as a gift and are willing to accept it. It could be our own need or it could be someone else's—as simple as the need to feel a tender hand on the shoulder or to receive a smile or a kind word. Sometimes we tend to go about in our own cocoon and don't recognize some of the pain, some of the needs that are all around us. When we are sensitive to that and accepting of the gift, the joy is there. I am living proof of this.

Postscript

Rev. Jim Rosemergy is an author and inspirational speaker, having spoken to enthusiastic audiences throughout the world. He has written 11 books including *The Transcendent Life, A Closer Walk With God*, and most recently, *The Prayer That God Prays*. Rev. Rosemergy currently serves as minister of Unity of Fort Myers in Florida.

When I recently contacted him, Jim offered the following: "There are events in our lives that transform us. Many of them come upon us seemingly with little opportunity for choice. The event happens, and then we have decisions to make. It is relatively rare to be able to make a choice that creates an event that is life transforming. The donation of a kidney to Carl Osier was one of those rare opportunities.

"I often think of Carl and, when I do, I send a thought to his new kidney with a blessing for it to continue to bless Carl, a wonderful God-centered man dedicated to service to the human family. It is difficult to determine the full impact of saying *yes* to the opportunity to donate a kidney, but one thing is clear; I am more sensitive to opportunities to serve and give than I was before. Saying *yes* to an opportunity to give can change the giver as well as the one who receives."

26

PRAY FOR OTHERS

I pray, knowing that my loved ones are filled with the life and joy of God.

Centered in the presence of God, I bring to mind my family members, friends, co-workers and others I am holding in prayer today. As I begin to pray in a spirit of thankfulness, I know that even before I have spoken a word, God's guiding, healing, prospering work has already begun.

"Dear God, thank You for Your infinite spirit that is expressing itself in and through these special people. If there is need for healing, I know that Your healing power is already active within them. If an illusion of lack has caused anxiety, I know that Your abundant supply is always present and fulfilling every aspect of their lives.

"With Your continuing guidance, my loved ones are filled with life, joy and love. They are joyful, healthy expressions of Your love."

Before they call I will answer, while they are yet speaking I will hear.—Isaiah 65:24

Preview

I spent almost all my time as editor of *Daily Word* at Unity Village, one of the most beautiful, peaceful places I have every been. Sometimes, however, I would travel to participate in Unity events or meet Unity friends. On one such trip to Washington State, I had the privilege of spending time in the home of Joel and Cynthia Abrams.

I felt right at home with this gracious couple, visiting with them, their son Micah and Cynthia's sister and mother. After dinner I wanted to hear more about Cynthia and Joel's experiences in helping their son Micah overcome some debilitating effects of autism. I was amazed and inspired as Cynthia told me the story of their journey of faith, as I believe you will be also.

Our Journey of Faith

By Cynthia Abrams

Observing my 9-year-old son fixated on a record going round and round on a turntable, I knew there was so much more of him waiting to break through his blank stare. There were love and intelligence that somehow could be unleashed. Discovering how to draw out these inner qualities was a journey of faith and perseverance for my husband Joel and me. Thank God, there were wonderful, dedicated people who joined us on our journey: my mother and father, tutors, and many of our friends.

Thirty-eight years ago, when I was pregnant with Micah, I started Unity classes with Rev. Margarette Meyer in San Jose, California. I learned about *Daily Word, Unity Magazine* and the Silent Unity prayer ministry, and they became an important part of my spiritual growth that I continue today. With my introduction to Unity, my life became one of prayer and meditation that gave me the strength to be there for my son.

Early on, we noticed that Micah could not hold his head up quite right, and he seemed to have a lazy eye, which was constantly off center. He never crawled, just scooted, but began to walk at 13 months. By age 3, he could say only a few words, never forming a sentence, and his behavior became like that of a "terrible two."

Joel and I took Micah to one doctor after another: none could diagnose what was wrong. They said he had minimum brain dysfunction, was legally blind in the left eye, and had poor vision in his right eye. Yet his IQ was in the normal range for his age.

Although Micah wasn't diagnosed with autism until he was 18, there had been early indicators. When Micah was 9, he attended a special school. An aide told us that she believed there were indications that Micah might be autistic. He would fixate on a spinning object or knock down the same toy over and over. He wouldn't listen to anyone.

I felt so frustrated because there seemed to be no answer as to how we could help Micah. Rev. Meyer encouraged me to search within my own soul for strength: "You know that you know the truth about Micah." She encouraged me to give life the light touch, which meant: bring all into the light of God. She told me to smile when the doctors said things such as "Micah will never learn to read," or "If he does, he won't understand what he reads." She said, "Never let a word of negativity about Micah take up residence in your mind. Let it flow over your head and past you. Rely on your inner spirit, for it is pure and one with the Truth."

New Hope

In 1980, when Micah was 9, we moved to Munich, Germany, where we found a wonderful tutor. Ermgard Pick was our saving grace. She told us about a patterning program one of her students had gone through. This boy had had a quarter of his brain removed and was in a state of nonawareness until he went through this patterning program. He improved so much that he was able to attend special education classes and walk using a walker.

Joel and I drove to Verona, Italy, to learn more about this program. During the week we were there, Micah was evaluated by a team that included a neurologist, family counselor, therapist, physical therapist and occupational therapist. Joel and I were trained in the program. They sent us home with a regimen of exercises and a special diet for Micah. Joel was more than skeptical about the program actually working.

Having only been in a foreign country a short time, we needed to find volunteers to help us carry out this program. Even before we started, however, special equipment had to be built. My dad, who was a carpenter, flew over from the States and built the equipment, exactly to specifications: a patterning table and overhanging ladder. Then my mom came to help us for several months.

Micah had an international group helping him: German, French, Welch, American and Portuguese. It took five people, one at each limb and one working at Micah's head. We would move his body as if he were swimming in a basic crawl pattern. This exercised his eyes and body at the same time, telling the brain to make a new connection.

Moving Forward on Faith

Thanks to what I had learned from Unity, I moved forward on faith. Joel thought the program was a bit hokey until one day he noticed that Micah was improving. Joel came running from Micah's room, shouting "It works! It works!"

Micah did everything we asked of him—wearing Velcro on his feet as he walked on a pad, he learned to lift his feet so that he would walk, not shuffle. He used the overhead ladder, gaining two inches in his chest and the ability to breathe deeply.

Micah got progressively better and better. We were amazed at how fast his vision and breathing improved. His vocabulary increased by leaps and bounds, and he talked in a stream of words.

As we were riding in our car one day, I said, "Oh, Micah, look at that beautiful rainbow!" He looked and said, "That's not a rainbow. That's a sunbow." "Yes, you're right, Micah, you're right. That is a sunbow."

We did two sessions five hours a day, six days a week. After ten months, we were told that Micah had come as far as he probably would with the program.

The next step was to involve Micah in sports activities—basketball, swimming and tennis—or to learn to play a musical instrument. When we moved from Munich to Hong Kong, Micah began tennis and swimming. These kinds of activities would continue to reinforce the connection between his body and brain.

A Gift

We moved to Washington State in 2004. A few years earlier, Micah received a gift he had wanted for a long time: a tiny fluffy dog. Little did we know what a gift from God Micah's dog Jack would actually turn out to be.

Micah had had epileptic seizures for years, so we kept a monitor in his bedroom. On the third night after we brought Jack home, the dog paced back and forth, back and forth. I knew he was uneasy about something. After a while, we went to bed but later were awakened by Micah's moaning: he was having a grand mal seizure. We felt sure that Jack's pacing earlier in the evening had been his sensing that the seizure was about to happen.

Jack has developed that gift over the years. He sleeps on our bed now, and when Micah has a seizure during the night, Jack will fly off the bed and run to Micah. If he doesn't wake us up when he bounces off our bed, Jack returns and barks until we do wake up. When we go to our son, we find Jack licking his ear, which seems to bring Micah around more quickly. Another blessing is that Micah's seizures have become less and less frequent.

Micah is now 37 years old. He reads, understands what he reads, and loves to share his knowledge with others. His favorite interest is cars: he has read all the brochures of the different makes. Micah knows the year, type of engine, and the special features of every car.

Our life with Micah has been an adventure in faith. Joel and I start each day anew, hoping for improvements, but happy with the status quo. We continue to love him and know that God's goodness provides our every need and opens the way for us when there seems to be no way. We know that we know the truth: Micah's spirit was, is, and will forever be perfect and whole.

Postscript

After growing up in San Jose, California, Cynthia met and married her husband Joel in Greece in 1966. With the birth of their son Micah in 1970, they continued their travels and lived in several countries. The Abrams now reside in Washington State and continue to advocate for autism. Cynthia says she feels privileged that "Our Journey of Faith" was published in an April issue *Daily Word* to coincide with Autism Awareness Month.

People who know of the Abrams' story have encouraged Cynthia to expand on it in a book. Cynthia is now writing a book that she hopes will be of help to parents and other caregivers of children with autism. She says that their dog Jack is still doing a great job to alert Joel and her that Micah is having a seizure, which at times can be as many as one every hour over a 24-hour period. Cynthia says, "Jack will keep a vigil until we tell him it's okay to leave Micah."

Micah's interest in cars now includes the hybrids along with the regular BMW!

27

SING

My prayer is a song of praise, flowing from my heart.

Mornings when I awaken to the glad songs of birds are joyful beginnings to my days. I can awaken every day with a song of joy in my heart when I am aware of God's presence and the blessings that come from knowing this truth.

Giving voice to my joy in song gives my thoughts and words even greater energy. A song can express a deeply held desire and resonate in my heart as a prayer. Through the music of my heart, I affirm the blessings I wish to see become evident. Each heart song is a song of thanks to God for guiding, loving and strengthening me.

But I will sing of your might; I will sing aloud of your steadfast love in the morning. For you have been a fortress for me and a refuge in the day of my distress.—Psalm 59:16

Preview

No matter how far away we were from the Gulf Coast of the United States during the last week of August 2005, most likely our attention and prayers were for all those who had lost their homes and possessions, family and pets to Hurricane Katrina. Eighty percent of New Orleans was flooded as the storm surge breached one levee and then another.

Just three years later in June 2008, I spoke at the Unity Church of Metairie's 30th anniversary celebration. In August 2005 all residents of Metairie, which is adjacent to New Orleans, had been forced to evacuate after this community was devastated by the wind and flood damage of Hurricane Katrina. Many who had been members of the congregation in 2005 had permanently relocated—especially those with young children in school. The church had been repaired, but some of the congregants had not seen one another since Katrina. I was blessed in being there to see their joyful reunion. Despite all they had been through, these wonderful people were joyful, giving thanks that they had not only survived but had also decided to stay.

Daniel Nahmod, a Los Angeles singer/songwriter, was inspired to visit New Orleans right after the devastation of Katrina. Like many others at that time, he was a good Samaritan who cared about and for the people who were left homeless by the flood. He was there when they needed a gentle touch and hope in starting to rebuild their lives.

A New Life—A New Song

By Daniel Nahmod

A little more than 10 years ago, I experienced an awakening. As a computer programmer, I had sat at my desk, more or less pretending to work. I did this day after day until one day I realized the life I was living was a life I no longer wanted to live.

Moving from Chicago to Los Angeles in 1998, I began my new life as a singer/songwriter. Soon after I arrived, I volunteered at Cedars-Sinai Medical Center with my guitar in hand, singing for patients, nurses and administrators. I sang for people in comas and watched as they moved to the rhythm of the music. Elderly patients would hum along to familiar songs.

I come from a family that suffered terribly in the Holocaust. So it's no accident that the intention of my music is to heal divisions, hatreds and fears. I don't claim that a song can change the world. But I've seen how the music and the message can make walls invisible for a few minutes at a time.

In 2005, just after Hurricane Katrina, I received a call from my friend, Rev. Richard Rogers, now of Unity of Naples Church in Florida. We talked about how we might be of help to the people of New Orleans and the Gulf Coast.

We met at the Houston airport and drove to the Houston Astrodome, where thousands of displaced people filled this gigantic building. They were people without homes to go to, without a job to report to, without a structure to their lives. Richard walked the floor shaking hands, hugging people, offering comfort. I played my guitar and sang songs during two of the most intense and profoundly heartbreaking days I have ever experienced.

The fear and absolute bewilderment were palpable. As I walked from cot to cot, in the middle of the most chaotic, disruptive, disturbing scene I'd ever witnessed, I stopped frequently to talk with individuals. I came to one elderly woman sitting on her cot, holding her head in her hands. A little girl, her granddaughter, was sitting by her.

"Would you like to hear a song?" I asked. She waved her hands in the air as if to say, "Whatever." I sat down next to her and said, "Would you do me a favor? I think you're going to know this song. Close your eyes and sing it with me."

I started playing "What a Wonderful World," and she began to sing ever so quietly with me. Her eyes were closed and so were her granddaughter's. I closed my eyes as well, and for four minutes or so there was no Astrodome, no despair, no Katrina. There was just the beauty of that song . We were lifted up and transported—not physically, but emotionally and spiritually—to the safest place imaginable.

In those few moments, the work of my life gained greater clarity. I'm aware that when I sing a song, whether it's in a hospital room or a large auditorium, for four or five minutes I am sharing a vision. It's a feeling, an instinct and hopefully a wisdom. It's a drop of consciousness—a safe space.

As a musician, I don't believe it's my responsibility to change the world or even to change the person in front of me. My responsibility is simply to dig as deep as I can, feel as authentically as I can and to share my consciousness. Singing has become a way I pray. There is a place I go when I'm singing, a place where I feel every word as a vibration or energy or consciousness, a place of real peace and love.

I feel blessed that I can share with others by singing and writing songs. Yet I know if I were only to have sung "What a Wonderful World" with the woman and her granddaughter at the Astrodome, just that song would have been enough for a lifetime.

There are artists who sell more CDs in a week than I have in 10 years. What's important to me is to live well and do good work. The lyrics of one of my songs, "Last Song," state it this way: "Is the world a little more peaceful? Are oceans and sky a little bluer? Is humankind a little bit wiser about the good we can do? Does the sun shine a little bit brighter where before there was only rain? If so, then I'm glad I came."

Postscript

Daniel Nahmod shares his message of peace, love and compassion with audiences around the world. Daniel lives his purpose by sharing his music and message of peace and compassion, which he said have deepened in his life since publication of his story in *Daily Word*.

He recently performed a concert with the Portland, Oregon, Boys' Choir, where he spoke about the power of a song to touch people's hearts, to make a connection, to inspire and support. "During the concert," he says, "I was reminded unexpectedly of something my mother said to me when I was a boy. We were at a dinner party with several families. Midway through the evening, I sat down at the piano and started to play. Within a few minutes, everyone had gathered around the piano to sing songs. My mother pulled me aside later and said, 'It's a wonderful gift you have—making people happy with your music.' Thirty years later, I'm proud that I've made a career of doing just that."

"My latest leap of faith has been to release my 13th CD, *Time for Fire*, which is themed entirely around taking the big chance and daring to live the longed-for life. Leaps of faith—and the resulting profound moments of joy and service—have certainly been the story of my life."

28

WORTHY OF GOOD

**I am a spiritual being created by God
and worthy of good.**

The voice of wisdom leads me in overcoming any challenge
of the human condition. It flows as a sacred language of the
heart and soul that reminds me that, like all people, I share in the
inheritance of God's good—despite any perceived differences of
who I am or what I deserve.

Even one clear and discernable voice speaking the truth of
the worthiness of all humankind sparks a like response from the
hearts of many others. With such reverence, I have spiritual
insight that reveals the wonder of life. I see the true picture of
myself and of all humankind: we are spiritual beings created by
God and worthy of good.

*For I have not spoken on my own, but the Father who sent me
has himself given me a commandment about what to say and
what to speak. And I know that his commandment is eternal
life. What I speak, therefore, I speak just as the Father has told
me.*—John 12:49-50

Preview

How does a child who has been abused emotionally and physically rise above torrents of such assaults to believe in his or her own self-worth?

Dave Pelzer's story is one example that such an overcoming is possible. And his triumph over the extraordinary negativity that was heaped on him in childhood has been a touchstone for thousands to begin their own journey from the darkness of abuse into the light of love.

And it has also caused those of us who thought we were giving and receiving as much love as possible to understand that there is no limit to the love we can share with one another.

Our own and other children hold a special place in our hearts, and we want to do all we can to love, nurture and protect them. Learning of Dave's abuse in childhood will more than likely bring tears to your eyes, as it did for me; however, as you will discover, his story is a testament to the powerful love of God as it is expressed and received in both unusual and everyday circumstances of life.

Worthy of Love

By Dave Pelzer

As a child, I longed for my parents' love. They were both alcoholics, and after my father left our family, my mother turned her rage on one of their four sons. I happened to be that one.

My mother constantly blamed me for "messing up" and referred to me as "It." Her anger increased over the next few years as she hit me and denied me food. When I was 8 years old, she punished me by holding my arm over the burning flames of our kitchen stove.

Eventually I was so badly abused by her that I could no longer explain away the bruises on my face and body to my teachers or school nurse. At the age of 12, I was taken out of my home and placed in foster care.

My second wife Marsha was the first person to say: "God loves you, Dave. I love you too and I believe in you!" Hearing those words, I started crying uncontrollably. I felt the joy of being loved. This wonderful woman loved me—a man who for much of his life felt that he was unworthy of love.

Marsha and I began in a working relationship—at a distance. I lived in California, and she lived in Florida. She was working as the editor of a book I had written, and we talked over the phone daily. I began to open up to her in ways I had never been able to open up to any other person. We took baby steps in building a friendship and in building our trust in each other.

We met for the first time when I invited her to California. Ready to test the waters, we wanted to know if there was a possibility for more than friendship between us. Holding a single yellow rose, I met Marsha at the airport. She later told me that her heart was pounding so that she thought she was going to pass out. When she saw me, everything and everyone else faded away. Right then and there she said to herself, "This is the man I'm going to marry!"

She was right. We married, and she became the director of a company that I had just started. Our marriage was tested, because the money just wasn't there in the beginning. We placed our lives and ourselves in God's hands. Once the books started selling, we actually had an income.

My message in my books and in my talks is about resilience and responsibility. Many people have had tremendous issues in their past, but they have been resilient and responsible enough to leapfrog over them.

True, I was abused as a child. My mother would not let me speak at home, so I mumbled. Being resilient and taking the responsibility for my own life, I have written four best-selling books and I speak to audiences all over the country. I have learned Japanese and Russian, and I do stand-up comedy. Yet I believe in simply focusing on doing the best job I can do. My job is helping others know that they can turn their lives around also.

I check in with myself every day, praying that I am doing the right thing for the right reasons. I wish I could discover the cure for cancer or find a way to feed all the people of the world, but what I do is bring a message of resilience and responsibility to the arena of child abuse.

Parents come up to me at book signings and lectures and tell me that, after reading my book *A Child Called "It,"* they can't wait to give their kids a hug. Teenagers tell me that when they put the book down, they immediately go to their parents and say: "Mom, Dad, I love you! And I am going to clean up my room."

When I received the TOYA—the Ten Outstanding Young Americans award (the equivalent of an Oscar for good Samaritans)—I walked onto a stage in front of over 2,500 people and didn't know what to say. Someone had suggested that I accept the award using my flair for comedy by doing my impression of former

President Bush. When I opened my mouth to speak, however, I spoke from my heart, as me. And something like this came out:

"Ladies and gentlemen, I would be sorely remiss if I did not pay homage to the people who played such a vital role in my life. I wish to dedicate this award to my grade school principal, teachers and nurse, all of whom, on March 5, 1973, intervened and saved me from further harm. They risked their jobs, their livelihood, by speaking out to authorities about my being abused. They saved my life.

"I also want to dedicate this award to my social workers, who stood by me even though just hours before going to court I recanted every statement I had made about being abused by my mother. I want to recognize my foster parents, who taught me how to walk and to talk and encouraged me to be the best person I could be.

"If it were not for these people, only God knows where I would be today. People make a difference. And with that, ladies and gentlemen, let's observe a moment of silence and thank God for who we are and what we have—right now, today."

I had not planned to say all this, but I felt as if God had given me a message to share. After a moment of silence, I walked out of the spotlight and off the stage. The audience remained silent. Then there was thunderous applause. I knew they had heard the message: We can all make a positive difference in the lives of children.

I look back at my mom and our relationship and recognize it as the tragedy it was. I don't believe that people wake up one morning and decide to be alcoholics. Neither do loving, caring parents suddenly decide to beat their children. Desperate acts such as these leach out of people because of their unresolved issues.

My mom obviously had some unresolved issues that showed up in her as alcoholism, frustration and anger. Often child abuse is passed down from one generation to another, but I decided to leave this planet cleaner than I found it in my own childhood. I think we all have responsibilities as parents, spouses and members of humanity. I carried the cross of abuse during my childhood, but my son did not have to experience what I did.

Being resilient and answering the wake-up call to responsibility, I learned that I can have close relationships and that I am worthy of love. My wife and son are living proof of that!

Postscript

Dave Pelzer is a recipient of the JC Penney Golden Rule Award. In 1993 he was honored as one of the Ten Outstanding Young Americans and in 1994 as one of The Outstanding Young Persons of the World. Dave's books include these *New York Times* best-sellers: *A Child Called "It"* (nominated for the Pulitzer Prize), *The Lost Boy, A Man Named Dave, Help Yourself, The Privilege of Youth* and *Moving Forward*.

Dave continues to be an example of someone who lives his life with resilience, faith in humanity and personal responsibility. He honors those who have stepped forward to ensure the health and well-being of children. High on his honor list are teachers, social workers, foster parents, law officers and volunteers.

All who have heard Dave's story or been in the audience when he speaks are reminded that each and every adult can make a positive difference in the lives of children and other adults as well.

29

GRATEFUL

With an attitude of gratitude, I attract greater good into my life.

I am grateful for all the good in my life and aware that by being grateful I am attracting even more good to me.

Gratitude is more than just thankfulness. It is a deeper awareness that because God is present within every person and situation, ultimate good is also present.

As I begin each day both in the awareness that God is all-good at all times and with the assurance that I am one with God, I have the strength, patience and faith to face any situation. My gratitude increases with each prayer of faith and each acknowledgement that wherever I am, God is.

I thank God for this day and for all the good it holds in store for me and for those I hold dear.

Let the word of Christ dwell in you richly; teach and admonish one another in all wisdom; and with gratitude in your hearts sing psalms, hymns, and spiritual songs to God.
—Colossians 3:16

Preview

I find that having an attitude of gratitude is its own reward. I'm a bit embarrassed to admit that when I suddenly have to go without the usual comforts of life, I realize my attitude of gratitude needs to be refreshed. For instance, back home after a vacation of camping out for a couple of weeks, I remember to be grateful that I can flip a switch on the wall and light up the room, turn on the faucet and fill a glass full of water, and sleep on a comfortable mattress.

When I heard Brother David Steindl-Rast's story, I was inspired to celebrate gratefulness every day. While most of us don't live the monastic kind of life Brother David has chosen, I believe that in living our lives from an attitude of gratitude, we are truly blessed. And in the following story, Brother David gives us some practical applications of embracing a life of gratitude that we can all practice.

Living Life in Gratitude

By Brother David Steindl-Rast

As a boy living in Austria during World War II, I never expected to survive the daily bombings or the hunger that my family, friends and I were experiencing. If someone had told me back then that I would live to the age of 21, I would have found that as impossible to believe as my living to 150. People I knew were being killed daily, so why would I expect to survive?

As with any conflict, that war brought terrible experiences. In Vienna, by the end of the war, countless houses had been destroyed, and there was no food, no water, no electricity. Even the church had been badly damaged, and yet every day at the same time, the pastor came walking over the ruins to pray with us and bring us communion. This gave us a lasting sense of the tremendous stability and support a spiritual community can provide.

As I think back on that time, I realize that in spite of the war, I enjoyed a truly happy youth. I had a wonderful group of friends, young men and women, and we were full of life.

Towards the end of the war, I read *The Rule of Saint Benedict*, which set out the guidelines for Benedictine monks. One of the guidelines was "to keep death before one's eyes daily." This guideline was offered as a way of gaining a better understanding of how precious life was. When faced with the ravages of war, we choose to live in the present moment. I believe that living in the present moment with God is the essence of the spiritual life.

In God's Presence

As I continued studying *The Rule of Saint Benedict*, the idea of becoming a monk was not at all foreign to me. But as a young man, I was too distracted by other things—I liked girls, and I liked having fun.

Several years after the war, my family and I emigrated from Austria to the United States. Less than six months after we arrived, a friend told me about a Benedictine monastery that had recently been founded. I visited Mount Saviour Monastery in Elmira, New York, which was, at the time, a farm where the monks lived in tents. As a young man of 25, I found this kind of dedication exciting and stimulating. I joined the monastery in 1953, and I have been a monk here ever since.

The environment of the monastery makes it easy to live every moment in God's presence. We monks often say that we are not the strong ones; those who live in the world and live their lives in stressful, difficult circumstances are the ones to be admired.

The Practice of Gratefulness

Joining a monastery means commitment to an ongoing conversion. The turned-around life of monks consists in striving to shift the focus, moment by moment, from constant distractions to the ever-present now. Their joy is to be in the presence of God and to practice gratefulness in continual inner prayer.

I believe that everyone who discovers gratefulness as a spiritual practice will also experience a conversion. People have told me that when they wake up to the belief that everything is a gift from God, their lives are turned around. Before that conversion, they may have been complaining about life most of the time. Being grateful, they no longer take even the simple things in life for granted. They find that there is a gift of opportunity within even the most unappealing gift-wrapped package. Most of the time it is an opportunity they will enjoy. Sometimes, however, it's an opportunity to grow that may involve some growing pains.

I find that a helpful exercise in gratefulness is to create my own reminders of what I am grateful for. During a lecture tour in Africa, I discovered that drinkable water was an incredible gift. When I came back home, I put a sticker on my faucet to remind me that every time I turned on the faucet, I received the gift of water. Traditionally, a prayer before or after meals is a reminder to be grateful for the food and the fellowship of those with whom we share a meal. A prayer in the morning and reading *Daily Word* are reminders that the whole day is a gift.

One of the reminders I have used for decades is, in the evening, to write down one thing that I am especially grateful for on that day. I may repeat things, but to the extent that I can remember, there is something new every day.

We have to be careful, however, not to turn gratefulness into glibly counting our blessings. More than that, gratefulness is a deep realization that continues to grow. We start by counting our blessings with the purpose of realizing that every moment is a gift from God. Every time we breathe in, we receive God's blessing; every time we breathe out, we give back to God in praise and thanksgiving. Our gratefulness is shared with the people we meet through a smile, through a handshake, through a kind word.

The practice of gratefulness is a spiritual practice that transforms a person given to moping and complaining into a person radiant with joy.

A special bonus of gratefulness as a spiritual path is that it gives us immediate results. When we make up our mind that for the rest of this day we will be a little more alert to everything being a gift, by the end of the day, we will be more joyful. Nothing that we take for granted gives us joy. Whatever we are grateful for makes us happy. True joy is the happiness that doesn't depend on what happens to us; it is what naturally happens when we respond gratefully to life.

In his first letter Saint John wrote: "See what love the Father has given us, that we should be called children of God; and that is what we are" (1 Jn. 3:1). If I were to ask a Buddhist, Hindu, Jew, Muslim or Christian about gratefulness, each would say: "Gratefulness? That's at the heart of our faith!"

Gratefulness brings us the joy of knowing that every moment of life is a gift, which unites us all as brothers and sisters in the family of God.

Postscript

Born in Vienna, Brother David Steindl-Rast studied at the Vienna Academy of Fine Arts (M.A.) and the University of Vienna (Ph.D.). He began studying Zen in the 1960s and became a pioneer in inter-faith dialogue. In 1975 he received the Martin Buber Award for his achievements in building bridges between religious traditions. His books include *Gratefulness, the Heart of Prayer* and *Belonging to the Universe* (with Fritjof Capra).

Currently, Brother David serves as founding advisor of *www.gratefulness.org*, an interactive website with several thousand participants from more than 243 countries around the world. Brother David divides his time between periods of hermit's life and extensive lecture tours on five continents.

30

WORLD PEACE

With every loving thought, we contribute to global peace.

Observing life with my physical eyes only, I might think world peace is impossible. When I choose to see the world with spiritual eyes, however, I know world peace is simply a choice away for every individual on earth.

Today I choose to see the various peoples of the world and all leaders making decisions for the good of all humankind. I visualize each arena of conflict as an opportunity for growth and understanding to come forth. I hold loving thoughts of peaceful outcomes between individuals and among nations.

I give thanks for everyone who is contributing to the evolving consciousness of global peace enveloping the world.

While they were talking about this, Jesus himself stood among them and said to them, "Peace be with you."—Luke 24:36

Preview

I met Diane Brandenburg, a longtime *Daily Word* reader and friend of Unity, for the first time in 2006 when my co-worker Christine Jenkins and I visited her in Palm Springs, California.

I had learned from Christine that Diane was a passionate advocate of world peace and an accomplished painter. I wanted to make a good first-impression on this woman I had already grown to admire. The moment I met Diane, however, I felt at ease. I wondered: Why had I felt such an instant connection with her? Did I feel as if I knew her because Christine had told me so much about her? No, I decided, it was because I had felt a tug at my heart—as if I was reuniting with a member of my family.

Diane took us on a tour around Palm Springs, which included a stop in front of a heart-shaped house. She laughed and explained, "This was Elvis and Priscilla Presley's honeymoon retreat." Next we drove to Mount San Jacinto, where we took in views of this mountain's magnificent granite peaks. Diane explained that the indigenous Indian people considered the mountain holy ground. I understood because I felt a "wholeness" while standing at the base of this mountain.

Later in a sweet, private moment, Diane told me that I reminded her of her grandmother. She quickly added, "Not in age, but in personality and the lilac color you are wearing." What a great honor that was, and it was confirmation of what I had felt: we were family.

Sowing Seeds of Peace

By Diane M. Brandenburg

My husband Lee and I have been married for 55 years. Several years ago we were going through a difficult time in our marriage. During this same period, my grandfather passed away and several other people in our extended family died. I seemed to lose any sense of peace of mind. My mother could see that I was growing increasingly depressed and she gave me a copy of *Daily Word*. This magazine had been a source of comfort and inspiration for her over the years.

I was uplifted as I read the positive message each day and the poems of James Dillet Freeman. *Daily Word* pulled me through this time of depression by reinstating my Christian faith and giving me a tool to use in moving forward with my life. I think *Daily Word* possibly saved my life. That is a strong statement, but I believe it's true.

Whenever I have a difficult decision to make, I call the Silent Unity prayer ministry. A wonderful person comes on the line to pray with me. As I listen to the heartfelt prayers that are being spoken, I am able to release whatever is challenging me. Experiencing the presence of God in the moment, I know everything is going to be all right. I let go and let God.

Many times from the 1970s to the present, Silent Unity and *Daily Word* have been there for me as challenges arose. One concern was for a young person in our life who had drug and alcohol addiction problems. We loved this person so much, but we didn't have any answers, because we had never been in a situation like this before. I called Silent Unity several times, and always the person who answered my call prayed just the right prayer. I could feel that the spirit of God was working in our young friend's life. Our prayers were answered, and he is now doing fine.

Young people are very dear to my heart, and just before Easter one year, I was taking my granddaughter to the airport when I saw three busloads of young men who looked to be her age—19 or 20—being deployed to Iraq. I began to think and pray about what I could do to help bring about peace in the world.

The next morning I wrote a letter to Unity and enclosed a donation, requesting that *Daily Word* and the poem "Listening to Silence" by James Dillet Freeman be sent to world leaders. *Daily Word* has been there for me during crisis. I wanted its positive, peaceful message to also be a support for people in power who are making decisions that affect the lives of all of us—our children, grandchildren, friends, neighbors and our world.

Issues of *Daily Word* did go out to 747 people in leadership roles in our world, accompanied by a letter that let them know Silent Unity would be praying with them and for them as peace becomes a reality in our world.

I believe peace is a reality for each one of us as individuals; and because this is true, peace in the world is possible. As my mother often said, "A little seed sown here and a little seed nurtured there will grow and become something meaningful." We can each sow and nurture seeds of world peace—in prayer, in thought, in word and in action. As we do, we are preparing for a harvest of good for our world family.

Postscript

Diane and her husband Lee are proud parents of four children and grandparents of four grandchildren. Diane is a charter member of the Dr. Martin Luther King Jr. Library Council for San Jose State University. As an artist and a philanthropist, she seeks out projects that emphasize the care, education and development of young people.

At a recent Global Alliance conference in Costa Rica, Diane was there with over 200 delegates from more than 40 countries of the world. She says: "The conference was made up of people from Africa, Australia, Denmark, England, Japan, Romania, Sierra Leone and many other countries. It was exciting, heartfelt and rewarding to see, be with and talk to so many people who truly want to see an end to wars and conflicts. They are willing to dedicate their lives, resources and personal funding to bring about peace. I came home with more determination than ever before to do my part in advancing world peace."

31

SPIRITUAL POWER

God is the one Power and one Presence active in the world and in my life.

An essential part of my spiritual practice is the prayerful process of denials and affirmations. A denial states that nothing has the power to disturb my joy or stand in the way of God's love and goodness in my life. Such a statement clears away old, limiting beliefs from my mind and allows me to discover the blessings within life's apparent challenges.

After cleansing my thoughts of limitation or lack, I follow with positive affirmations of truth. I know that there is one Power and one Presence active in the world and in my life. I know and believe that all things are possible through divine love. Using denials and affirmations, I am actively transforming my outlook on life. Gone are any limitations to good. I am now open and receptive to the promise of my divinely inspired potential.

First clean the inside of the cup, so that the outside also may become clean.—Matthew 23:26

Preview

When challenging situations or circumstances occur in life, we may not believe that we have the strength, the faith and the capability to do all that is called upon us to do. Then someone is able to seemingly look within our souls and confirm that indeed we have all that is needed to stay strong and steady so that we are the parents or children, the spouses or friends that our loved ones need in the moment or for an extended time.

Several years ago I felt a lack of strength in being able to withstand my mother's decline into Alzheimer's disease. Although I had visited her almost every day for the 10 years she had been in a long-term care facility, Mother had forgotten my name. She had also forgotten how to eat on her own and was beginning to lose her ability to even swallow food that was fed to her.

One faithful day as I was leaving the Silent Unity building to visit Mother, I met Unity ministers Dorothy and Phil Pierson. Whenever we met, Dorothy always asked me about my mother. This day was no an exception. When I told her of Mother's declining condition, her response was about me: "You are being strong for your mother." "Oh, Dorothy," I replied, "I'm not strong."

Dorothy shot back a look that alerted me that she was going to say something I needed to listen to, and I did listen! "You are strong through the presence of Christ within you!" she affirmed with such assurance that I had to believe her.

I am so thankful for that "chance" meeting with Dorothy. She was right. Through the Christ within me, I knew that although Mother's physical body might be in decline, her spirit was eternal and free. And because I looked to Christ for strength, I was able to be strong for Mother.

The Power Within

By Rev. Dorothy Pierson

My father was studying to be a Presbyterian minister when I was born. Mother said he carried me around the house while reading the Bible. I don't remember my father because he died when I was 2 years old. I believe, however, that as he read the Bible with me in his arms, I was being programmed to be a minister.

I have always believed I came into this world with a mission. At first I thought it was going to be in the theater, but during my first year as a scholarship student at the Cornish School of Art in Seattle, Washington, I became very ill with tuberculosis. I spent the next two years in a tuberculosis sanatorium.

My treatment consisted of bed rest and fresh air. The first year I was not allowed to let my feet off the bed to touch the floor. The window in my little cubicle of a room was left open even in wintertime. Often when I awoke in the morning and emerged from the mound of blankets covering me, I would see that the water in the glass beside my bed had turned to ice overnight.

My mother came to visit me every week. With her sitting close beside my bed, I would close my eyes and remember the home where I was born. I would describe the rooms and furniture in such detail that I felt as if we were once again there together.

An Inner Strength

Life in the sanatorium was drastically different from the one I had enjoyed as an active teen who loved to play tennis and golf. Yet during this time of extreme isolation, I began to realize I had an inner strength, a power within that I draw upon to this very day.

This realization began when my aunt brought a visitor, Rev. Paul Rigby of the Unity church in Seattle. Almost immediately he took my hand in his and closed his eyes. Then he began to talk to the invisible life of God that was in every cell and atom of my body. I was absolutely thrilled as I literally felt my body begin to respond with healing to the life that he affirmed was present within me. From then on I looked within to the Source of Life for my healing.

Rev. Rigby brought me *Daily Word* magazine and other Unity literature. I believe the greatest truth that the Unity teachings have revealed to me is that God is not only around but also within each person. In the church I had attended, I had learned to pray to a God that was outside of me. When I learned about Unity, I found God within, and that understanding made a positive difference in my life and has supported me over the years.

I was healed of tuberculosis, but after having been in isolation so long, it took me awhile to come back to the world. One day my aunt encouraged me to go to the Unity center in Seattle to hear a speaker, Charles Fillmore, co-founder of Unity. I was rather devoted to my church, but my aunt explained that Unity never asked people to leave their churches or to become members of Unity.

So on a stormy day, I took a long streetcar ride from my home in West Seattle to the Unity center downtown. When I walked into the sanctuary, I heard Charles Fillmore speak these words: "Jesus Christ is now here, raising us to his consciousness." I had never in my life thought that Jesus Christ could be here right now.

Going Home to Unity

Donald O'Connor, a friend of mine, was interested in going into ministry. So he and I met Charles Fillmore the next day for a job interview. We wanted to work at Unity headquarters in Missouri. In my naiveté, one of the first things I said to Mr. Fillmore was, "Have you ever heard of *Daily Word* magazine?" His eyes twinkled a bit, and he said, "I think I have heard of that magazine." I continued to rave on about *Daily Word*.

A few months later, Donald and I received letters saying that we were both hired. That was over 60 years ago. I felt at home the moment I entered Unity Village, as if I had been called to be there by Spirit.

I worked in Silent Unity, which was so right for me. I met Frank B. Whitney, the founding editor of *Daily Word*, and May Rowland, the director of Silent Unity. Later when Martha Smock became the editor of *Daily Word*, we became very close friends. I loved sitting next to her in the Silent Unity healing meetings, experiencing the power of Silent Unity prayer. I remain dedicated to Silent Unity.

In Ministry

I was ordained in 1953, and the best thing I ever did was to invest myself in the young people through my work at Unity churches, first in Toronto and later in Honolulu and Seattle, where my husband, Phil Pierson, and I were co-ministers. I had no children of my own, but as a minister I had all these children in my life. I still hear from them today. They come up to me and say, "Thank you! You helped me so much."

In my ministry, I have taken Jesus' words literally: "No man cometh unto the Father, but by me." When people come to me for help, one of my greatest joys in life is to realize that every single person who comes to me has that Christ Presence within. I don't have to give people anything. These are divine appointments in which I silently call forth the Christ within as I pray with people.

The two-year period in that tiny room in the sanatorium was a time of knowing the truth of an old adage: "Muddy water, let stand, becomes clear." That's exactly what happened. I learned that I was clear within myself, where the spirit of God resides.

We are all clear within because the God Presence is within us. The God Presence knows us, loves us, heals us, guides us, prospers us—always.

Postscript

Dorothy Pierson is an ordained Unity minister whose inspirational writings and poetry have appeared in *Daily Word* and *Unity Magazine*. She and her husband Phillip were seen every week for many years on the popular television show *The Best Is Yet To Be*. A past president of the Association of Unity Churches, Dorothy continues to be involved in the presentation of Unity teachings.

When I met with her recently, Dorothy talked about her early days in Unity, but she was enthusiastic about having met Eckhart Tolle, speaker and teacher of spirituality. Dorothy pointed to Tolle's book *The Power of Now*, which lay on a table nearby, and said, "We can all live in the moment!"

"How do we know when we are living in the moment?" I asked.

"We are always in our right place at the right time to receive the word that is given to us. We are living in the moment when we *feel* it is the greatest moment we have known to this point. There are no worries; only the greatness of the moment."

I know without a doubt that being in the presence of Rev. Dorothy Pierson, I feel the greatness of the moment.

32

CAREGIVER

Thank God for caregivers who touch the hearts and lives of others in special ways.

Throughout the world, people are reaching out with a loving touch to children and adults who need care on special occasions or on a daily basis. The blessings that are given flow from the Christ Spirit within these caregivers, fulfilling a sacred responsibility shared by one creation of God with another.

And when I'm not able to be there to care for loved ones, I pray for them. I also pray for the ones who are providing the care needed. I envision a scene in which kindness and consideration, respect and reverence are both given and received.

Caregivers understand that they are serving God by caring for precious creations of God. They consider it an honor to give their time, to apply their knowledge, to share their faith in loving, helpful ways.

We were gentle among you, like a nurse tenderly caring for her own children.—1 Thessalonians 2:7

Preview

As I regularly watched local news anchor Elizabeth Alex, I sensed that she was more than a talking face relaying the events of the day. As she delivered the news—both the good and the bad—she conveyed an understanding of and compassion for people.

When, for several days, Elizabeth was missing from the nightly broadcast, I thought I had missed the announcement that she was on vacation. Then one evening her co-anchor shared that Elizabeth's husband had passed and told of the tremendous strength and courage that Elizabeth had shown throughout her husband's illness.

Several years later, I attended an awards ceremony where Elizabeth was the keynote speaker. Afterward, I approached her and asked if she would consider sharing her story in *Daily Word*. I was delighted when she said *yes*. I soon learned, however, that the story was not to be about her own family but about another family that she had become personally involved with during a critical time in their lives.

Helping Our World One Person at a Time

By Elizabeth Alex

In April of 2002, I flew to the Middle East to cover a story in which I became deeply, personally involved. As a news anchor for KSHB-TV in Kansas City, Missouri, I traveled with a photographer to Afghanistan. Dr. Gary Morsch of Heart to Heart International invited us to accompany him as HHI delivered medical aid to people there.

Just before we left Kansas City, some Palestinian friends asked me to go to the West Bank and Gaza to report on the story of how the people there were suffering. This was during the height of the suicide bombings in Israel and the siege of the Church of the Nativity in Bethlehem. The Muslims, Christians and Jews were all suffering. The residents of Gaza didn't have medicine or food. Dr. Morsch agreed that after a shorter stay than planned in Afghanistan, we would go on to Gaza.

In Afghanistan, I had seen so much horrible poverty and hope-lessness that I didn't know what to expect in the West Bank. On the flight in Tel Aviv, I sat next to a man who was praying using his prayer beads. I remembered that I had a tiny rosary in my purse. I took it out and began to pray.

As soon as our group left the plane, Israeli security guards stopped us for questioning. A misunderstanding erupted during the interrogation. Tension escalated, and one guard ordered us back on the plane: "You are going to Jordan and leaving all your stuff here." Dr. Morsch argued with him and finally told us: "Sit down. If they need to arrest us, let them arrest us." The plane to Jordan left with-out us, and we had time to figure out what we were going to do.

A thought popped into my mind: Even though my friend Susan lived back home, I knew she had connections in Israel and might be able to help us. I called my husband—1:30 a.m. Kansas City time—and asked him to call Susan. He did. Susan knew someone who worked in the Israeli health ministry and she contacted him and vouched for us. Nearly five hours later, we were finally free to go on.

We first visited Jewish children who had been disabled and trau-matized by the violence around them. We then hired a man to drive us to Bethlehem Bible College. About halfway there, military activity around us escalated. "It's too dangerous to go on!" the driver declared. We stopped and took refuge in a nearby hotel lobby.

A Dangerous Situation

While waiting in the lobby, we heard the sound of gunshots. Israeli soldiers had taken over the hotel we were in and were firing directly across the street, where the Church of the Nativity was under siege.

Needing to get back to Tel Aviv and feed video back to my station, we were finally able to hire another driver who would risk the trip. He drove slowly down the narrow streets with the car's caution lights flashing. All along the way, guns of soldiers were trained on us as we drove past. We finally made it back to Tel Aviv, where we were met by even more armed soldiers.

The next morning we drove to a Palestinian clinic in Gaza. We had a short time to take some video and do some interviews. Everywhere I looked, I saw distraught mothers holding malnourished-looking children. One mother captured my attention. She held a beautiful baby girl whose body was completely limp. This mother was walking around, hoping someone would help her. I asked the doctor in charge if I could interview her. He said, "Yes, if it's okay with her." While the doctor translated, the woman began to tell me her story. The three children she had had prior to this child had died. This little girl had been born with club feet and club hands. She had dislocated hips and was unable to use her legs. There was no hope for her ever walking without some kind of serious medical intervention.

I started to cry, which greatly surprised the doctor. Perhaps he had not expected American journalists to have feelings. As the interview continued, a bond of friendship grew between the doctor and me and between the mother and me. Her name was Intisar, and her daughter's was Doa'a, which means "prayer of hope." I left affirming, "Doa'a is going to have her surgery."

When I returned to the United States, I worked with Kansas Congressman Dennis Moore's office and with some wonderful people on the Jewish Community Relations Bureau in Kansas City—all were trying to help this Palestinian family. I contacted the U.S. State Department, completed paperwork, and searched for doctors and a hospital that would donate their services.

A few months later, Intisar, her husband, and Doa'a came to Kansas City. They stayed here for six months, while Doa'a had surgery and therapy that enabled her to walk and use her hands. She's come back twice for further therapy.

Helping Intisar

During the spring of 2007, Intisar's husband called Nick Awad, our friend here in Kansas City who spoke Arabic, to tell us that Intisar had been diagnosed with breast cancer. Of course, I wanted to help Intisar but wondered how I would find a doctor and a hospital that would donate very expensive, time-consuming cancer treatment for her. I asked a surgeon I knew from Medical Missions Foundation, and she offered to do the surgery. She contacted specialists needed for chemotherapy and other treatment. They all agreed to treat Intisar. The CEO at a local hospital offered his facility.

After a biopsy, it was determined that Intisar, who was 35 years old at the time, had an extremely aggressive form of breast cancer. Although she had a life-threatening, allergic reaction to her first chemotherapy drug, they found one that worked for her. After having chemo and surgery, Intisar is now cancer-free.

A Dream Come True

During her mother's treatment in Kansas City, Doa'a was able to go to school. This had been one of her dreams. Doa'a was 6 years old—so tiny she wore size-four clothes. When I took her shopping for school clothes, she found a jumper she really liked. She looked at the jumper, which was a size six, saying, "Elizabeth, this one is good!" When I put it on her, she didn't come close to filling it out. When she looked at herself in the mirror, however, her big brown eyes shone brightly. She twirled around in front of the mirror as if to say, "I'm a school girl at last!"

I believe God put Doa'a and her family in front of me, questioning, "What are you going to do for them?" When I took that first step to try to help, so many other people came forward—Christians, Jews and Muslims; doctors, politicians and friends—to help my Palestinian family. Everywhere I turned, somebody knew somebody else who could do whatever needed to be done. It has been miraculous.

As a news anchor, sometimes the only thing that I can do is put people's stories on the air and let other people decide what they can do to help. Other times, however, I can help. A while back, I was in Kansas Senator Sam Brownback's office covering a news event and told him about my Palestinian family. The senator reminded me of something Mother Teresa had said: "If you can't feed a hundred people, then feed just one." I believe that we can each make a difference by helping one other person. It's a good feeling, and one person after another, we end up helping our whole world.

Postscript

Elizabeth Alex is an award-winning news reporter and evening news anchor of the *NBC Action News*, Channel 41, in Kansas City, Missouri.

When I recently contacted Elizabeth, she told me that she couldn't believe the number of responses she had received about her story in *Daily Word*. She had heard from people across the country. Some said that they were touched by Doa'a's story. Others were pleased that Palestinians were highlighted as friends and that attention was brought to those who were suffering and in need.

Elizabeth went on to share the following:

"Today Doa'a and her family are surviving. They remained safe during the latest war in Gaza, although for a time they had 40 displaced relatives living in their small house.

"My goal is to bring Doa'a back to the United States again for occupational therapy that will help her to write and to also dress and feed herself. Her resiliency is amazing. She and her brother and sisters still attend school, which is a privilege for them. Her family recently called me on my phone at work. Doa'a left a message that she loves me. I shall always love her too."

33

DIVINE PURPOSE

I love what I do, and I do it with purpose.

As I reflect upon my talents and interests, the activities that bring me joy and fulfillment, I realize that these are the things that give shape to my purpose in life. And each one is a gift from God, meant to be developed and shared.

Each new day, I welcome the opportunity to put my spiritual gifts into practice, to grow them and expand the blessing that they are. I confidently share my talents with the people around me with commitment and enthusiasm. When I love what I do and do it with purpose, I am a blessing to the world.

I am a unique and divine expression of Spirit. My life is filled with purpose and meaning as I develop and share my spiritual gifts with others.

Do not neglect the gift that is in you … put these things into practice, devote yourself to them, so that all may see your progress.—1 Timothy 4:14-15

Preview

I have admired actress Rhonda Fleming for many years. For a short time in a darkened theater, I would let my imagination transport me onto the movie screen to experience the romance and travails of this beautiful redheaded heroine.

Although I didn't know much about her personal life, I felt she had something to share that would be welcomed by the *Daily Word* family. When I called her about being featured in *Daily Word*, I learned that she was member of our family of readers. As we talked, her story unfolded, and I found even more to admire about her. Rhonda has an inner beauty that shines on others to help them through some of the most trying times of their lives. She not only cares about others but also cares for others, making sure that those who need medical or financial help receive it. She is a real-life "action hero."

God's Purpose for My Life

By Rhonda Fleming Carlson

At age 14, I was drawn to the call of the beach far more than my assignment to dissect a frog during science class. Planning to ditch school that day, I wore my swimsuit under my clothes as I left home. Two of my friends decided to come along for a swim.

There was no one else at the beach when we arrived, which should have been a clue of rough waves. "I'm gonna beat you!" I yelled as I ran into the water. I had swum a ways when suddenly the water was sucked out from under me and I was standing in sand.

Stunned, I looked up to see a 10-foot-high wall of water coming toward me.

One of my friends yelled, "Swim out! Swim out!" But I just stood there, frozen to the spot. The wall of water came crashing down on me, whirling me around and around. My feet went up, and I couldn't catch my breath. My life hadn't been that long, but it all flashed before me: I thought of my sister, my mother and the rest of my family. Then once again, I was dropped onto the sand long enough to take in a deep breath. I lost consciousness when the second wave crashed over me. When I awoke, I was back on the beach; by the grace of God, my two friends were able to rescue me.

Divine Assurance

I believe that surviving this experience and several more life-threatening accidents over the years was the assurance that God had a purpose for me. At age 18 I had written a poem in which I asked God to help me give purpose to my life. I know that God honored my request over the years, although at times that purpose seemed to grow out of the loss of the very people I loved the most.

I was born and raised in Los Angeles, California. My mother and dad divorced, and my mother, a former model and actress on Broadway, raised me. My father died relatively young at age 53. I had a wonderful older sister, Beverly, who was my best friend.

My career as an actress began as a Hollywood Cinderella story at age 15. I was discovered by an agent who saw me as I hurried to high school one day. I grew up in the Hollywood studio system, which took total control of an actor's career. My first featured role was in the film *Spellbound*, which starred Ingrid Bergman and

Gregory Peck. I went on to do some 40 other films. I didn't feel, however, that by focusing on my career as an actress I was fulfilling that higher purpose I had prayed to fulfill.

When my sister Beverly was diagnosed with ovarian cancer, I knew I was to be there with her, to help her throughout her treatment. We were both scared at times with no one to talk to us or give us any information in order to understand her needs. For instance, just after she received chemotherapy, I took her home with me, but I did not know how to help her. I was heartbroken to see that her needs were not being met. In learning what Beverly went through, I learned how to help other women.

I saw the need for a place where care, compassion, communication and concern were all a part of a person's treatment. I believed that clinical social workers could help alleviate the fear and uncertainty of the one who was told she had cancer. All kinds of helpful information could be made available as well as support groups to offer hope. I felt such a need for a place where there would be tender, loving care for women and their families.

Thirteen years ago, along with my husband Ted Mann, I started the Rhonda Fleming Mann Clinic for Women's Comprehensive Care. About a year after that, we founded a resource center for women with cancer. Eventually, I opened a shop called Reflections that had everything that's needed for these women: prostheses, wigs and turbans. In this one shop was everything that my sister and I had to traipse all over to find for her.

Tender, Loving Care

I told Beverly, not long before she died, "We are going to have a place where all the tender, loving care that you and I didn't have will be available to women." And she said, "Oh, honey, I'm so glad. Just always, always make it a place of hope."

And that's what we did because Beverly always had hope. We read *Daily Word* together every day; we lived with it. She had it with her day and night in her purse, and it gave her such hope. She survived many more years than she should have with ovarian cancer. She never said the "C" word. She'd say, "Come on; I'll feel better next week. Then we'll go to lunch." It was her amazing courage and strength that encouraged me to move forward and help others.

Another turning point in my life was when my husband Ted was dying. My dad, my sister and my mother were gone.

Ted and I did not share the same religious beliefs: he was Jewish, and I, Christian. Sometimes he would go with me to church. He would stand up and sing all the wonderful Jesus songs and loved it. I got such a kick out of it. But the thought of losing him left me with such an inner starving. I got on my knees and said, "God, I'm lost. Please take over my life. Help me through this difficult time." And God did help me be there for Ted. I read the 23rd Psalm to him as he peacefully passed from this life.

It is interesting how God has continued to help me. Darol Carlson, whom I'd met 35 years earlier in Sacramento where he was in business with my sister's husband, came back into my life. His beautiful wife of 50 years had died three years before. Darol and I read the Bible together, we pray together, we attend prayer groups together. The togetherness that Darol and I now share as husband and wife is a blessing from the Lord.

Our faith in God and the miracles of God have blessed us. When my energetic, active husband suddenly had a stroke, we, along with hundreds of others, prayed our way through a dark time, believing in an all-powerful God who created us to live a life of abundance. Thank God, Darol has made a miraculous recovery. I'm grateful to the Lord.

What I have learned in life is that every one of us has a purpose: to put God first and then, in whatever good we do, give all the glory to God, who, as my dear mother always said, is our best friend.

Postscript

Rhonda Fleming Carlson starred in more 40 films, including such classics as *Connecticut Yankee in King Arthur's Court* and *Gunfight at the OK Corral*. Rhonda supports many philanthropic and humanitarian organizations, including P.A.T.H. (People Assisting the Homeless) and Childhelp USA.

She is the recipient of numerous awards, including two in 2008: the Caritas Award from Saint John's Health Center and The Irene Dunne Guild and the Lifetime Achievement Award from Concordia University. Rhonda continues on in her dedication to improve the lives of others.

Learning that this "Queen of Technicolor" is the subject of a new paper doll book brought back memories of times I enjoyed playing with paper dolls when I was a child. Of course there were hours of cutting out clothes, but with that done I had all I needed for many more hours of entertainment. Times have changed and the toys of today have great technological features that I never dreamed of as a child. It's good to know that paper dolls are still available—I suspect as much for adult collectors as for children at play.

You can visit Rhonda at *www.RhondaFleming.com.*

34

CHANGE

I cross every bridge to change with faith and confidence.

As I complete one phase of my life, I make ready for the next one. I may be changing from a role as a student to one of being an employee. I may be taking on the added responsibility of owning my own home. I may no longer choose the single life and commit to a lifelong partner.

Whatever change I embark on, I build a bridge to my new experience. With planning, insight and prayer, I trust as I step forward to change. Prayerful reflection is a spiritual component to my bridge of change. I know what is mine to do because God's love and wisdom are guiding me.

With faith and confidence, I trust that there is a time and a season for each change. Following divine guidance, I am secure as I cross each bridge to my next destination.

For everything there is a season, and a time for every matter under heaven.—Ecclesiastes 3:1

Preview

Like me, do you feel uncomfortable at times making a change in your routine? I have tended to sit in the same seat when taking a class, the same row in church and the same chair at my kitchen table. More than likely, this did not make me a smarter student, a more enlightened congregant, a more satisfied diner.

In fact I've read that when people make a small change such as brushing their teeth with the left hand when they normally do it with the right (and vice versa) they are enhanced mentally. Of course there are the big changes in life: moving, marriage, divorce, retirement and other events that can prompt us to take a wrong turn and think of all that might go wrong rather than all that could go right. How can we avoid doing this?

Whether we are preparing for or right in the midst of a change, reading Joan Borysenko's story will help us plan and accomplish the best from any changing circumstances in our lives.

Saying YES to Change:
The Anatomy of Spiritual Transformation

By Joan Borysenko, Ph.D.

Many people are fearful of change, both the expected and unexpected kind which they need to experience in order to live life with greater freedom and happiness. Like the acorn that has to die in order to be reborn as an oak tree, we are all in the midst of being transformed. With that transformation, we can become more compassionate, caring people who offer our unique gifts in the service of a larger whole. Change offers us the possibility of growing beyond our perceived limitations to the fullness of our divine potential.

The mysteries of change are known in every world wisdom tradition and provide us with an archetypal map for spiritual growth. In the book *Saying Yes to Change: Essential Wisdom for your Journey*, my husband and co-author, Gordon Dveirin, and I outline the three classical stages of change that constitute a rite of passage—for instance, from the acorn to the oak or from the caterpillar to the butterfly.

First, change entails separation from the old life; second, it ushers in a threshold period of not knowing what's next; and finally, it paves the way for a return to the world strengthened and transformed. So if you're in the midst of an unwanted change, rather than thinking of yourself as an unwilling victim, think of yourself as an initiate of the journey of the soul, which will bring you solace as well as wisdom.

The Three Stages of Transformation

1. Separation: The Journey Begins. When I directed a mind/body clinic at a Harvard Medical School teaching hospital, patients often told me that the day they were diagnosed with cancer or AIDS, they died to who they were. They felt as if they were falling into an abyss.

When illness, job loss, financial reversal, betrayal, divorce or death of a loved one disrupts our world, our ego identity shatters and we are separated from what was. The human response is fear. At a deeper level, however, a spiritual process is beginning to unfold. The shell of ego cracks, and its habitual way of constructing the world falters. Deprived of familiar frameworks, we are invited to enter the ritual process of transformation.

2. Dwelling at the Threshold: Surrendering to the Unknown. The late anthropologist Victor Turner, who identified the three stages of transformation, termed the second "the time between no longer and not yet." We have died to who we were, but are not yet reborn to who we might become. We are at the doorway, the threshold of new potential.

When the Israelites escaped from slavery in Egypt—which in Hebrew means "the narrow place"—they had to wander in the desert for 40 years. We all go through narrow places where we're challenged to let go of old beliefs and habit patterns that limit us. It may take time for them to surface and for us to let go of them in order to heal. The journey across this desert is not one in which we hurry. This is the great unknown where ordeals are faced, allies appear, and the gifts of trusting in and surrendering to a larger divine reality are claimed.

3. The Return: Transformation and Rebirth. The caterpillar who died to itself in the phase of separation—then dwelled at the threshold in its chrysalis—is finally reborn as a butterfly that can spread beauty and inspiration with its very presence.

Our spiritual transformation entails dying to the false-self with its fears, attachments and need to control. With the rebirth to our true nature, or God-self, we are in alignment with a larger whole and we truly support the inner freedom and well-being of all. The strengths discovered in the second phase of our transformation are powerful gifts that we bring back for the good of family, community and the world.

Whether it's an unwanted circumstance that happens to us or something that we initiate voluntarily, change is an invitation to actualize the wisdom and compassion that make us both fully human and evident manifestations of the divine. Life, after all, is a journey into the unknown where change is constant. The challenge is to pay attention, heal what needs healing, and grieve what we've lost as a testimony to how precious it has been.

Staying faithful to the certainty that we live in a spiritually meaningful reality, we are called by change to authentic trust and surrender. Answering that call, we live in peace, joy and service right now in this beautiful and holy world.

Postscript

Receiving her doctorate from Harvard Medical School, Joan Borysenko is a trained medical scientist and a licensed psychologist. She is the director of the Claritas Institute's Spiritual Mentor Training Program, and the author of numerous books and audio programs. Her book, *Saying Yes to Change: Essential Wisdom for Your Journey*, was co-authored with her husband, Gordon Dveirin.

Watching and reading the news of local and global events can leave any of us with a sense of hopelessness if we let it. As a distinguished pioneer in integrative medicine and a world-renowned expert in the mind/body connection, Joan offers us hope with a wake-up call to the spiritual dimensions of life.

Just reading the titles of her books gives me hope. I especially like this one: *It's Not the End of the World: Developing Resilience in Times of Change*.

You can visit Joan at her website, *www.joanborysenko.com*.

35

FOCUSED

I am divinely focused and spiritually fulfilled.

What is on my mind and heart to do, to experience today? Every day I am learning as I go, collecting information, trying different approaches. However, as I pray my way through each circumstance and each day, my focus is on divine guidance.

Being divinely guided, I have the perception and understanding that bring all into focus. Everything I consider takes on a new clarity. I make adjustments to the way I think and comprehend, seeing the greater possibilities that are always awaiting my acceptance, rather than accepting any seeming limitations.

My life takes on new meaning and purpose as I contribute my thoughts and energy toward the fulfillment of my soul.

I believe that I shall see the goodness of the Lord in the land of the living.—Psalm 27:13

Preview

In the 40 years I served at Unity, I was blessed with co-workers who not only believed in prayer but also practiced it. Each employee who chose to participate had a prayer partner during a special month of prayer at Unity. We would meet for about 30 minutes a week to support each other, all who called on Silent Unity for prayer, and the world itself.

I had wonderful prayer partners over the years, but having Kimberly Morrow as my prayer partner came with a bonus: the added company of her guide dog, Fern. We usually met in Kimberly's office, and Fern would be off-harness. All employees had been instructed not to distract Fern when she was in-harness and helping Kimberly along her way from one place to another on the Unity campus. This was an instruction we all found difficult to follow. It took all I could do to hold back from saying something to this beautiful black Labrador or from stroking her noble head.

Once Fern was in Kimberly's office and off-harness, however, I could give her my attention. And she acted like the typical Lab, lavishing me with wet kisses and trying to jump into my arms. Once she quieted down, prayer time began. Every once in a while, I would look at Fern lying near my feet. When she would lift her head a bit to look at me, I saw such assurance in her big brown eyes. I knew that—in her silent way—Fern was joining Kimberly and me in prayer.

I See God Clearly

By Kimberly Morrow, Ph.D.

At age 35, I consider myself to have been blessed with a life that has already been wonderful beyond all measure. I have had the privilege of acquiring a good education: I graduated from a large, suburban high school and went on to earn B.A. and M.A. degrees and a Ph.D. I have been gifted with a tremendous "cheering section" of family and friends.

I have had the privilege of seeing God clearly from a unique vantage point few others are fortunate enough to share. I have never seen the mountains, but can well appreciate the struggle of the climb. When I scan a document in braille, I have the extraordinary sensation of truly being physically touched by the power of words. Listening to a friend reading a text aloud to me, I revel in my narrator's words. The basic elements of his or her true character inevitably take center stage through the distinct interpretations that spring forth from the tone, quality and inflection of a well-modulated voice. The textures and shapes of stones and seashells, the tides of the ocean, the smell of freshly mowed grass and the songs of unseen birds fill me with a sense of wonder and mystery. All comprise remarkable pictures of nature that I believe are every bit as vivid to me as are rainbows, skies and sunsets to those who are sighted.

Beyond the Visual

Perhaps the most rewarding aspect of living in the nonvisual world is the fact that certain judgments that have become all too commonplace in the everyday lives of most people who can see rarely enter my awareness. I can know an acquaintance for months, have a cup of coffee and sit directly across from that person, or take his or her hand in mine and never have an inkling of the race or ethnicity of the person with whom I am sharing a portion of my life's journey. "Foreign" accents are simply another element of interesting, nonvisual texture in my auditory landscape.

I will never in my life comprehend the reasons why the mere color of one's skin or one's nation of origin has caused barriers to be erected throughout the course of history.

On a daily basis, I rely on others to describe the moon and stars, sun and clouds—things I have never seen but that I know perfectly well are present. And just as I have always taken these elements of nature for granted, so have I also taken for granted the existence of a higher being in the universe. The presence of God is simply one more thing I have never seen but which I can sense in every fiber of my being.

My existence is also devoid of the visual images that often accompany humankind's concept of God. It is amazing to me that, while we are outwardly visual creatures, gaining about 80 percent of our sensory information by means of sight, we build temples, sing songs, create religious dogma, all to worship a Being we have never seen.

The experience of spirituality in general is one in which we may focus on physical healing, but God heals in other ways. There is healing of the mind and soul too—a healing from the inside out. Even though I am not what many would call physically healed, I have been healed in other ways and been given so many other gifts. God has healed me by giving me a type of sight—insight.

A Companion and Guide

I have a guide dog named Fern, whom I love dearly. Fern allows me to travel more quickly, confidently and safely. She is trained to stop at steps and curbs, to cross streets from curb to curb, and watch for oncoming traffic.

People who raise guide dogs instruct the puppies in basic obedience commands. The dogs are returned to the school at approximately 18 months of age, where they are instructed in "harness commands." The handler works his or her guide in harness using commands such as left, right, straight and forward. Guide dogs are not expected to memorize routes; instead, the blind handler must be aware of his or her environment at all times and must instruct the dog as to the direction in which it should go.

Although being blind comes with its fair share of trivial inconveniences, and although there is much in the world that will always remain a mystery to me, I can state with complete conviction that I would not trade my life for that of anyone else. To have been bestowed with vision beyond vision is an experience that defies description. I see God clearly, and when it comes right down to it, what more could one truly wish for?

Postscript

Kimberly Morrow earned her B.A. from Baker University with a double major in German and Spanish. She went on to earn an M.A. in Germanic languages and literatures from the University of Kansas and a Ph.D. from the University of Kansas in educational policy and leadership. She enjoys creative writing, technology, knitting, herb gardening, singing and playing piano and dulcimer. She resides in Overland Park, Kansas, with her third working guide dog, Fern

Kimberly serves at Unity World Headquarters in the Message of Hope department—the department that distributes Unity books and literature free of charge to the blind and to those in prisons, hospitals and health-care facilities.

"Message of Hope is such a fabulous place to work," says Kimberly. "It is immensely gratifying to hear the excitement in people's voices when we are able to provide them with a word of encouragement they can access easily. To these wonderful individuals, we truly do serve as a message of hope."

36

FREEDOM OF SPIRIT

I am free in mind, body and spirit!

The freedom to travel and move about from area to area, country to country, does come with some rules and restrictions. Sometimes, too, delays happen, schedules change, and other routes and means of travel must be taken.

Spiritual freedom, however, has no limits. I can choose how I fill my heart and mind. I can choose how I experience God, how I pray, and how I practice the presence of God in my daily life.

Embracing freedom of Spirit, I break through any self-imposed limitations and open myself to divine possibility. By choosing encouraging words, uplifting thoughts and positive habits, I give full expression to my spiritual freedom.

For you were called to freedom, brothers and sisters.— Galatians 5:13

Preview

Fear of the unknown can keep any of us stuck in unchallenging situations and unfulfilling circumstances—if we let it. When we allow ourselves the spiritual freedom to forge ahead on to those previously unknown and untried pathways of life, however, we experience more of the wonder of life.

Until I was in my 50s, I had convinced myself that I could never learn to swim. Several people had tried to teach me to swim, but I was unable to get past fear in order to believe that I could. One day when I was in my friend Kay's pool, in the shallow end, I was showing her that I couldn't float. I would sink as soon as I started to lie back in the water. Kay then said something that surprised me: "Do you trust me as a friend who wouldn't let you go under?" "Well, of course, I do," I said, not too convincingly. She then asked me to lie back on the water and relax, letting my feet float to the surface. "I promise, I'll keep your head above water." I did trust her, and I found the courage—even for a few moments—to show her that I did. And to my surprise as I lay back and relaxed, I floated like cork!

Later I took lessons with a couple of other friends and learned to swim. It would be great to be able to say that I am now a long-distance swimmer, but I'm not. Yet releasing fear and having the courage to swim the length of a pool is a great accomplishment for me. I'm really a great floater. I think I could float on my back for hours. It's a wonderful feeling of freedom.

In her article, Dr. Judith Orloff offers some steps that will lead us on the path of being courageous and emotionally free. She explains that through her own life-lessons, she came to understand that emotions are not meant to be a form of torment that makes a person feel miserable. "They can be a springboard to the higher self," she says, "which is always compassionate and loving."

Courageous and Emotionally Free

By Dr. Judith Orloff

As an assistant clinical professor of psychiatry at UCLA, I see myself as a bridge between traditional medicine and the spiritual, intuitive realm. I profoundly believe that it's important to integrate the wisdom of both in order to help people and to help myself.

My mother was a powerful teacher for me in a certain way. She, too, was a physician. During the 1940s, she worked in a hospital emergency room in Philadelphia, but ironically she struggled with self-doubt that kept her from seeing her own magnificence.

Although she had been a fantastic, loving family physician for 40 years, at age 70—with a thriving Beverly Hills practice and flawless credentials—a part of her felt unworthy of such success. In order to prove herself and keep up with younger doctors, she decided to take her National Medical Board Exam again.

Mother's preparation for the tests required months of intensive study. My father, who was also a physician, and I were spectators, loving her the best we could and hurting as she hurt. During the board exam, the lymphoma that she had been diagnosed with 20 years earlier suddenly changed into an aggressive malignant leukemia. She passed her exam, but she died shortly after.

Taking a Spiritual Path

As a young doctor myself, watching as Mother let fear, anxiety and self-doubt accelerate her own death was extremely difficult for me. Yet I recognized that, over the years, I had developed similar traits of being a workaholic and having self-doubt. This recognition prompted me to take a different path, a spiritual path, on my own life's journey.

On this path, I learned to transform negative emotions, such as self-doubt and fear, into something positive. I came to understand that emotions are not meant to be a form of torment that makes a person feel miserable. They can be a springboard to the higher self, which is compassionate and loving.

Early in my career, however, I was unsure of how I might bring what I had learned to help my patients. I had a patient I will call Christine who I was treating for depression. I prescribed antidepressants, and she got better. Then during one session with her, I suddenly had a premonition that she was going to attempt suicide. Afraid to trust my intuition and scared of what other physicians would think if I brought intuition and spirituality into my practice, I didn't broach the subject of suicide. Within a week, Christine overdosed on the antidepressants I had prescribed.

Christine survived, but this was a wake-up call for me to have the courage to go beyond the realm of traditional medicine. I began to incorporate intuition and spirituality into Christine's treatment. She stopped being hard on herself, emotionally beating herself up by thinking she wasn't worthwhile. She developed more self-compassion and continued to improve. She saw fear differently than a biochemical abnormality and embraced it as an opportunity for her to be courageous.

Our Opportunity

We, too, can discover that fear is an opportunity to find courage and that frustration is an opportunity to find patience. Anxiety can prompt us to find inner calm, and loneliness alerts us to be more connected to others. Releasing anger, we bring forth compassion.

In pairing negative emotion with positive change, I teach people to start with a less-than-intense fear that they want to be free of. I ask them to identify the fear. It could be a fear of saying no to a friend. Once they work with that, I suggest, "Now go to a larger fear, such as a fear of being a failure. Identify what triggers the fear, what sets it off." Perhaps it's seeing the careers of friends skyrocket while they themselves feel as if they will never achieve what they desire to achieve.

Once the trigger has been identified, I ask them to look at that fear from a spiritual perspective. Allowing ample time for the answer to each of my questions, I continue: "Ask yourself, How can this fear help me develop courage? Can you see that having courage means that you will cultivate self-love and build confidence in the talented person that you are? Define what courage means to you. Then deactivate the fear by becoming still, closing your eyes, and connecting with Spirit within. Repeat this statement: 'Spirit within me is greater than any fear. I am not my fear, I am larger.' Begin to understand what a tiny speck on the screen of your life that fear is."

Any one of us can accomplish the spiritual shift of going within and tuning in to Spirit. When we do, we realize that we have the strength and courage to deal with anything or anyone because we are not alone. We understand that Spirit is moving us beyond the small self to the courageous self. This is the core of emotional freedom.

Transforming Our Emotions

We can have an epiphany, a life-changing revelation, but I believe in taking small, steady steps in transforming our lives. It's with stitch by golden stitch that we become beautiful tapestries of soul development. A three-minute compassion meditation once or even several times a day helps us tune in to our spirituality and follow inner guidance, transforming our emotions.

Such a meditation might go like this: "Close your eyes and take a deep breath. When any thoughts come to mind, release them and let them float away like clouds drifting across the sky. Return your focus to your breath often and then begin to focus on your heart—everything that is loving and good and compassionate within you. Relaxed and at ease, allow yourself to feel all the compassion within and for yourself."

Whenever any of us start embarking upon an emotional healing, it's critical that we devote time to such a "compassion practice" in order to be able to deal with whatever we are going through—whether it's self-criticism, depression, anxiety or frustration.

As we work on the development of our souls, we are able to see that every heartbreak, every loss and every gain can transport us to a life of greater courage and emotional freedom.

Postscript

Judith Orloff, M.D., a psychiatrist and medical intuitive, is author of the *New York Times* best-seller *Emotional Freedom: Liberate Yourself From Negative Emotions and Transform Your Life*. Her other best-sellers are *Positive Energy*, *Intuitive Healing* and her first book *Second Sight*. *Second Sight*, which has been rereleased, is being considered for an ongoing dramatic television series based on her life.

Dr. Orloff has received an outpouring of positive feedback from her books and her story in *Daily Word*. People told her how grateful they were for her help in dealing with fear and negativity during stressful times. They appreciated that the connection between emotional freedom and spirituality was brought to light. "Connecting with a loving higher power is essential for emotional freedom," she says. "We then can overcome any adversity we face." Dr. Orloff continues to encourage people to develop spiritual muscles when dealing with their emotions so that they won't be pulled down by negativity even though it is intense. For more information and inspiration, visit *www.drjudithorloff.com*.

37

I SURRENDER

God, take my life and use it.

Dear God, here I am. Take my life and use it. In complete surrender I turn myself and all that concerns me lovingly over to You. Create in me a clean and perfect heart.

Take my will and mold it according to Your divine will. Teach me Your ways. Teach me Your paths. Lead me in the truth and teach me. Teach me to love all that is good with all my heart, all my soul, all my mind, all my strength.

Teach me to love as You love—pure and unconditionally.

Take my life and use it, dear God. Make of me a perfect channel through which Your loving, healing, harmonizing power may flow, to uplift and to bless everyone whom You bring into my life.

In complete faith and love, I commit myself to Your will and Your way. Take my life and use it in Your service.

Make me to know thy ways, o Lord; teach me thy paths.—
Psalm 25:4.

Preview

The year before I retired as editor of *Daily Word*, I had the privilege of attending an international *Daily Word* and Silent Unity conference at Unity Village. I met associates from Argentina, Australia, Canada, Costa Rica, Dominican Republic, England, Germany, Ghana, Guyana, Jamaica, Mexico, New Zealand, Nigeria, The Netherlands, Trinidad and Venezuela. These devoted people provide Silent Unity prayer support and *Daily Word* magazines in their respective countries. All the associates involved remain devoted to blessing people with affirmative prayer and a daily message of inspiration.

Different languages were spoken at the international conference, but the love we shared with one another did not need to be translated. It was palpable.

Laura Bermeo is responsible for *La Palabra Diaria*, a translation of *Daily Word*, lovingly prepared for our Spanish-speaking family in Costa Rica. Although Laura Bermeo's story had been published in *Daily Word*, I met her in person for the first time at the conference. When Laura and I came face to face, we embraced as though we were family.

And indeed this is true, for we are members of the Unity family who share a passion for and a dedication to our sister publications: *Daily Word* and *La Palabra Diaria*.

Surrendering to God

By Laura Bermeo

I was reading all the self-help material I could get my hands on, but my life continued to spiral more and more out of control. Gino, my 11-year-old son, had run away to the streets of San Jose. He lived in the red zone—an area filled with crime and poverty. A friend who was aware of my dilemma handed me a business card with the Unity-Costa Rica address on it and said, "This is a place where you will find the help you need."

I followed my friend's advice, but when I first began attending Unity, I didn't believe that the good news they shared could possibly be true for me. I continued attending because in my heart I knew I needed to understand that I was a child of God and that God's presence and power were within me.

Overcoming My Past

I was alone and in need of the basic necessities of life; however, my attempts to find work had failed. My self-esteem, energy and resourcefulness had evaporated. My coping skills were gone. The events that had wounded me in childhood came back to haunt me. Old feelings of complete abandonment returned.

My brothers and I had been victims of abuse. Sometimes we had searched through the trash of wealthy neighborhoods just to find food. I still held a vivid image of myself as an 8-year-old, sitting on a bench and listening as my father told me, "Take care of your brothers, because your mother can't." Ten years would pass before I would see my father again and that was for one last time.

My relationship with my mother was traumatic. When I was 11 years old, she took me to a hotel where she had already sold me as a prostitute to an old man. We stood outside the building as I cried with the deepest pain and told her, "Mom, please! I don't want to do this!" Without saying a word to me, she returned the ill-gotten money, took me by the arm, put me in a taxi, and sent me home.

I believe she suddenly saw the horror of her own childhood reflected in me and had compassion for me. Many years ago, her mother had sold her to a man; but there had been no empathy or rescue for my mother. I am thankful to her for the decision of love she made for me just in time—a decision only God could have guided.

A New Way of Life

As an adult attending the Unity church, I was learning that God was with me and within me, already present and available. I began to replace my negative thoughts with life-affirming prayer. I called the Silent Unity prayer ministry in Costa Rica every day and asked everyone I knew to pray for Gino.

I looked for any opportunity to be at the Unity church, a place where positive people and principles nurtured me. I volunteered, helping to set up church services and distribute bulletins. I eventually helped out in the children's program. Unity minister Juan Enrique Toro started a two-year leadership program that I completed, and I was later hired as the prayer director's assistant. With an income, I was able to pay for food, a place to stay, and other essentials.

As I continued to study and attend classes, I learned two powerful teachings—one of prayer and one of surrender. These continue to be the pillars upon which my life is sustained.

I realized that the only thing I could do to bring my son home was to surrender him to God and continue to pray. Finally, after three months of prayer and complete surrender, a great emotional weight was lifted from me, and I felt at peace.

The very next day, I received a message from Gino: "Mom, I want to come home. Please meet me at the bus stop." Feeling both relief in the present and hope for the future, we made a commitment to start life anew.

Seven years have passed. I am very proud of Gino and thankful for our relationship, knowing all the problems we have conquered. He now lives with me, takes painting lessons, and has returned to high school. We attend family counseling together, and we hold God's hand as we continue to learn, heal and surrender.

The transformation I have experienced began through Unity teachings. Unity is, indeed, my spiritual home. As I began to understand spiritual laws—that giving is as important as receiving and that God is our sustenance—I started giving and volunteering. Giving, when you have a surplus to give, is relatively easy. But when you have only enough to buy a loaf of bread *and still give*, I believe giving becomes an even greater commitment.

Now, as current director of our prayer ministry, I work daily to maintain the ministry, managing people and procedures. We are now publishing *Daily Word* in Costa Rica. I continue to heal my life by putting to use every blessing God gives to me. The wonderful result is that I am happy giving to and trusting in God.

Postscript

Laura Bermeo is the director of Costa Rica's Unidad En Oración (Unity in Prayer). Laura's son Gino is her main assistant in this ministry. Laura gives spiritual counseling and volunteers for Siembra, a home for homeless teenage girls. She created Regala Libertad, a program that raises funds to make *La Palabra Diaria*, *Daily Word* in Spanish, available to those in prisons in Costa Rica. Laura is currently writing her autobiography.

When I asked Laura if she had received any comments about her *Daily Word* story, she said: "Yes, the majority of responses were from mothers with problematic sons. The article was both a comfort and wise consul for them." She continued: "My son Gino and I are doing very well. Gino is working at a full-time job while completing his studies. He is still his mother's son and will always be so."

38

TRANSFORMATION

**A divine transformation is taking place,
and a new me is emerging.**

Today is a day so full of potential for my own personal transformation. My life is already an example of transformation. From childhood to adolescence to adulthood, the ways I look, sound and think have changed. I've grown and matured physically and mentally. In an awareness of my indwelling presence of God, I am unfolding spiritually as well.

I follow the higher purpose in life that God is always calling me to fulfill. Seeking, first and always, divine guidance and understanding, I live from the inside out. Divine inspiration directs my thoughts, words and actions. Through the sacred presence within me, a divine transformation is taking place, and a new me is emerging.

*Listen to me, you that pursue righteousness, you that seek the
Lord. Look to the rock from which you were hew.*—Isaiah 51:1

Preview

Physical transformations are, for the most part, visible and apparent. Over a few years, a child becomes a young adult. We may have been close by to see this transformation happen over time or be amazed when we are reunited with the adult who seems only to resemble the child we once knew. Or we may notice that, after several weeks of being dedicated to a healthful lifestyle, which included nutritious food and plenty of exercise, a friend's weight-loss is evident.

There is also the kind of transformation, however, that can happen in an instant. This is not one that requires willpower or a long period of time; it is the result of our God-power used to overcome the seemingly impossible. Once we tap into the power of God that is inherent within every person that has ever been, is now, or will be, we are transformed. That transformation may be freedom from a drug dependency or freedom from being haunted by anything that keeps us from living life fully in the moment.

No matter what our own personal transformation may be, in the following story, Rev. Leo Booth reveals how we can all live a spiritually rich life.

Moments of Transformation

By Rev. Leo Booth

I have found that one of the most helpful practices one can develop is to be aware of the moment, particularly those moments of awakening to who we are. This awareness brings about transformation.

Such a transformation happened for me in 1977. I was living in England, the land of my birth, going about being the Episcopal priest I had trained to be. Then I had a car accident. In the moment of that car accident, I was able to really see myself as I was. I emphasize the word *see* because I think that it's a very powerful, spiritual word about perception. In that moment, I saw myself as other people saw me. In other words, I saw myself drunk, unmanageable and powerless.

My new perception led me to treatment for alcoholism and to a spiritual transformation.

I've heard people say that their moment was when they woke up in jail or realized that a child they loved no longer wanted to be around them. Perhaps they had been in denial about themselves and how they were living their lives.

Some people's experience is about having lived in an abusive home. Rather than staying in the negativity of that abusive home, however, they've been able to see and experience a goal that is the opposite of that abusive home.

Not everybody's story involves alcohol or the loss of everything or everybody of value. All human beings have a history, and the history that they have is experience—experience they can use for their personal transformation on their spiritual journey.

Spiritual Recovery

My moment of knowing that I wanted to change opened the door for me to live a life of sobriety, move to the United States, develop a ministry that deals with spiritual recovery and healing, and become a Unity minister.

When I had the car accident, I was led to the question: "What is my personal definition of spirituality?" I understood that spirituality was about being positive and creative. I then began to consider what life experiences I could use for the benefit of myself and other people, while serving the God of my understanding as well as I possibly could.

Many people who have experienced abuse have written books with information and encouragement that offer hope and healing to others who have been abused. They have looked at their lives from a place of courage and decided there is a positive alternative.

Most of us are forced into change and transformation by circumstances in our lives that we are not comfortable with, circumstances that are creating pain. In this sense, pain becomes a spiritual aid because pain tells us something is not right. If we didn't have that pain, we might stay in the problem, rather than moving on to the solution.

My experience of pain was fundamental in my transformation. First I recognized I didn't want to continue to live as I had been living. And second, I was willing to seek help at a hospital for three months. The hospital was only a building, but the recovery began when I went there. My willingness to look at my life and make some changes made a difference.

I prayed and meditated. I also listened to the stories of others and was willing to identify with those stories rather than see everybody as different from myself. Everybody has to face challenges; it's how we overcome those challenges that strengthens and transforms us.

Our Stories

All the stories of the great myths—whether Greek, African or Asian—basically revolve around a very similar theme: On the journey of our lives, how we face a challenge and then overcome that challenge gives us the lessons we need for our transformation. With perseverance, we maintain the path, maintain the journey, maintain the teachings we have accepted.

About six years into my recovery, I began to understand that there is a difference between spirituality and religion. A person's religion is a denomination, what most people are born into. Spirituality is much more of a choice. With spirituality, we use our religious experience to move to the next level and recognize what we all have in common; it's the inclusiveness of the spiritual life.

Spirituality is always about connection. It's about living the positive and creative spiritual message of being connected and inclusive. The great men and women who are spiritual leaders bring us a message of unity and inclusiveness.

We are transformed in moments of living the truth of our spirituality. I like to use the analogy of the cartoon character Popeye and his spinach. When Popeye was in a difficult situation, he would reach for a can of spinach. Eating the spinach instantly gave him the strength to overcome the challenge. The spinach was always there, but Popeye left it to the last minute. I always wondered: why didn't he reach for the spinach earlier? Why did he wait until he was beaten up or nearly drowning in the ocean?

To me, spirituality is a little bit like the spinach: it's always there, but sometimes we don't reach for it or realize that it is there. We are going through difficult times because we are not reaching for the spirituality that is in our back pocket.

God's spirit is always there within us. This means that there is always a solution, always a positive and creative message. But we need to reach for it, and the reaching for it is getting into recovery or letting go of a destructive relationship.

That power is always within us, because the spirit of God is always within us. By the way, it's not just within us. We can also reach it through other people and by reading the Bible and other inspirational writings. We can receive it from music or theater.

We can because, wherever we look in this world, God's all-powerful presence is there.

Postscript

Rev. Leo Booth is an internationally acclaimed author, lecturer and trainer. He holds a master's degree in theology from King's College, London, England, and is a Certified Addictions Counselor and a Certified Eating Disorders Counselor. Rev. Booth presents workshops, lectures and training on a broad spectrum of issues and has appeared on such television shows as *The Oprah Winfrey Show*, *Geraldo* and others.

He continues to remind us that transformation is a process. "It's up to the individual to do his or her part," he says. "We can make choices, take action and accept responsibility for our health, finances and relationships. The good news is that because divine power is within us, we can change destructive habits and ways of thinking."

From his work as both minister and an addictions counselor, he has developed a new spiritual model based on Choice, Action, Responsibility and Empowerment. Visit his website: *www.fatherleo.com.*

39

INNER PEACE

Centered in God, I experience absolute peace.

Storms may rage on the surface of an ocean, but deep below, the waters are calm. The fish know to stay in that peaceful place and let the storm pass.

In prayer each day, I choose to turn my thoughts to the peace of God within me. On the surface of my mind, the appearance of lack or conflict or fear may toss my thoughts about in worry. I gently release those thoughts and move my attention deeper, to a place of peace within me.

I take time for prayer throughout my day. As I rest in the stillness, I am serene—mind, body and spirit. Each time I center myself in the peace of God, I experience absolute peace and tranquility.

The promise of the Lord proves true; he is a shield for all who take refuge in him.—Psalm 18:30

Preview

I've heard the theory that a person can seem to be a different person to each person who knows him or her. I believe this includes but moves beyond the roles that tend to define us, such as our titles as members of a family, organization or community. We are all works in progress, so we are growing and learning from one experience to another, from one day to another. How we responded to a challenge or opportunity one day may be different than how we do so the next day.

And think of actors who may change characters in one acting role after another. Who would have ever guessed of the turmoil stirring within the soul of actor Michael Learned when she was staring as the serene mother of the Walton family on TV? Yet how she found her peace and her identity as a spiritual being is a most inspiring story.

A State of Peace

By Michael Learned

At the time I was offered the role of Olivia on *The Waltons*, a family TV drama that aired in the 1970s, I had hit rock-bottom. I was drinking too much, and I felt lost. My life was a stark contrast to the idyllic scenes portrayed by Olivia and her family. The path that had led me to this point began with a childhood that was enchanting in some ways and confusing in others.

I was the oldest of six girls in my family. My father worked for the government, and we moved many times during my growing-up years. During our travels, I was exposed to different cultures, languages and beliefs. My parents were charismatic, interesting people who were a little overwhelmed with being parents. They taught us to have good manners, but they didn't quite let us be children.

We curtsied when we met people and stood up when an adult entered or left a room. This became a rather comical routine whenever my parents had an argument. When my mother became angry and raced out of the room, my sisters and I would all stand up. Just about the time we would sit down again, my father would leave the room to find her, and we would all pop up one more time.

When I was 12 years old, we moved to Austria. We were there for only six months when my parents sent me off to a boarding school in England. After winning the drama cup my first year, I studied drama there for the next three years.

By the time I was in high school, I was in the United States and had been to so many different schools that I lost interest in studying—but not in boys. At 16 I participated in a Shakespeare Festival in Connecticut, where I met and fell in love with Peter, another aspiring actor. Immediately my parents shipped me back to England, but when I came back to the States a year later, Peter and I married.

By the age of 24, I had three sons and was trying very hard to be the perfect '50s wife and mother. Peter came home early one day and surprised me. I was so upset with myself: I started sobbing because I hadn't had time to clean the house, take a shower, get the kids cleaned up, and have dinner ready.

Our generation didn't talk about feelings or problems. Peter and I did have problems, and eventually we divorced. By the time my kids hit their adolescent stages, I was 32 and didn't have a clue about who I was.

A Closer Look

I was doing theater in San Francisco, acting in a play called *Private Lives*. It was a big hit, and we were going to be taking it on tour. As a single parent, I knew I wasn't making enough money. My agent had told me that the producers of *The Waltons* were looking for someone to replace Patricia Neal, who played Olivia Walton in the initial movie. I didn't want to work in television, I felt I was wrong for the part, and I was terrified of the Hollywood scene. I did have three children to support, however, so during a two-week hiatus from the play, I reluctantly went to L.A. to audition. I stayed in a little hotel with a bottle of bourbon for strength and a Raggedy Ann doll for comfort.

During the audition, I felt as if I were in a fog. I was in so much emotional pain. Even so, I landed the role. I believe God was watching over me and leading me.

Being cast in *The Waltons* helped financially, but I was drinking too much, and I knew I had to take a good, hard look at myself. When I did, I discovered my co-dependent ways. I had spent my life either trying to please other people or trying to manipulate them into doing what I wanted them to do. Whatever illusions I had about myself had been shattered.

I decided to get sober, and that's when I began an incredible spiritual journey. I went to my ex-husband's isolated cabin on the California coast. There I faced the fear of being alone for the first time in my life.

During my 10-day stay there, I walked along the beach observing the pounding surf. I silently watched herds of elk and white-tailed deer. One foggy day, I was lying on the beach, more relaxed and at peace than I could ever remember being. As I ran my fingers through the sand, I was amazed at all the tiny, different colored pieces that made up the sand.

I thought about how humanity is like the sand. We as individuals are tiny cells that make up the whole. We each have a role to fill and our own spiritual journey to complete. And as we do, we contribute to the health and wholeness of humanity.

That day on the beach, I transcended fear and concern during a time of meditation. I reached a state of peace that I had so desperately needed and tried to achieve through alcohol. I didn't know whether I had meditated for a second, a minute or an hour, but I knew I was filled with incredible bliss.

Discovery

Mine has been both a wonderful life and a painful one. At times I felt as if I were at the bottom of a slimy well, trying to crawl out. Sometimes I would even get to the top of the well and then just slide right back down.

I married for a second time, and again there were problems. By this time, I had learned that I couldn't help this man unless he wanted to help himself. I am a great believer in prayer, and when I prayed to God to remove the challenge from our marriage, my second marriage broke up. Although I don't advocate divorce, I don't believe I could have made it out of that well of fear and confusion while still in that marriage.

My experiences in life helped me grow as a human being. I was willing to go through more pain to get out of the pain. Discomfort can be a motivator for growth. I have changed, but I still try to help people who want to be helped. I just don't "over help."

I haven't had a drink in over 25 years. I met a wonderful man who loves and accepts me just as I am—even with my character defects. John and I have been married for 14 years. My three sons are grown and married, and I have five grandchildren. I am a happy, settled person now.

My life is so wonderful today that it is beyond anything I could have ever imagined. Still, I keep praying, asking God to keep me in check so that I don't take any blessing in my life for granted.

Postscript

Michael Learned is the recipient of four Emmy Awards for "Best Actress"—three for *The Waltons* and one for a later series *Nurse*.

Some may have thought that her original billing as "Miss Michael Learned" on *The Waltons* was a result of ego or a demand, but nothing could be further from the truth. She was unknown to the public at the time she won the role of Olivia, and her billing was to keep the audience from being confused about her gender.

The girl, who at age 11 left the family farm in Connecticut, has become a world-renowned actor. However, if today one would ask her what her greatest accomplishment in life has been, I believe she would say it was not found on stage or screen, but on the beach that day when she discovered and started to live from the peace of God within.

40

WORK IN PROGRESS

The light of Spirit is shining from me in generous, kind and loving ways.

I place certain expectations on myself as I aspire to be an expression of Spirit in my world. My intention is to be generous, kind and loving, but from time to time, my actions may fall short of such goals. Perhaps a family member and I have exchanged unkind words, or maybe I've been acting as though I woke up on the wrong side of the bed.

Thankfully, I know that God always supports me. I am a work in progress, and with this day, I'll have another chance. Centering myself in God's love, I am drawn to speak words that uplift. And if I find myself needing an attitude adjustment, I spend some moments in gratitude, which bring me back into an experience of joy. The next breath, the next word or the next encounter is another chance to let Spirit's light shine from me in generous, kind, and loving ways.

Our inner nature is being renewed day by day.
—2 Corinthians 4:16

Preview

I was distracted by my own thoughts for a few moments when I first met Sally Halford. I found it difficult to picture this soft-spoken, demure woman sitting across from me as ever having been a prison director, but indeed this was true. I had heard of the Kansas Correctional Institution at Lansing, where she had served. This prison had been the home of several notorious inmates who had been portrayed in movies and TV.

It only took a few moments of listening to Sally speak, however, to understand the strength in her gentleness and the power within her prayers to bring out the good in people whom it seemed, all the world, except her, had given up on.

Sally's story challenges us to move beyond the facade of what a person appears to be and to see the good that is within, waiting to be expressed and shared.

Everyone Deserves a Second Chance

By Sally Halford

Even now I remember how I felt as a sad and confused little girl at age six. My mother and father had divorced. The father I adored was no longer in my life. My mother was distraught, continually wringing her hands and crying, not knowing how she could raise my three brothers and me on her own.

I missed my dad. Every time I heard the rumblings of a truck on the road outside the country school where I attended first grade, I would run to the window and wave, hoping it was my dad. I would always come away feeling brokenhearted because it wasn't him. He had abandoned my family and me.

Thank God, a neighbor sent me a subscription to *Wee Wisdom*® magazine from Unity, which gave me a second chance at life. In fact, I believe the teachings featured in this children's magazine, once published by Unity, may have saved my life. Reading *Wee Wisdom*, I understood that God's spirit was within me and could be expressed as me in wonderful, powerful ways. I knew I had a choice in how my life could unfold. Unity has been an influence in my life for more than 50 years.

I am now retired after a long career in the corrections field, during which my Unity background sustained me. As a director of several correctional facilities, I offered inmates a second chance at life.

At the Kansas Correctional Institution at Lansing (KCIL), where I was director, we began a new program where both men and women were housed in the same minimum security prison. I was excited about this program because I knew that inmates who served long terms without ever talking with or being around those of the opposite sex were doomed to fail in society once they were released.

At KCIL, male and female inmates had opportunities to relate with one another during supervised, structured activities such as self-help programs, educational classes, dances and team sports. The men and women had rooms, instead of cells, in dorms at opposite ends of the campus. Some inmates were able to leave during the day to work at a local factory. All in all, it was a proving ground before they were deemed ready for release from the state prison system.

The new program was still proving itself when an inmate, we'll call him John, entered the program. He was a tall, muscular man, a loner who never smiled or talked to many people. John did form a kind of puppy-love relationship with another inmate, a beautiful young woman. We'll use the name Sarah. When another inmate flirted with Sarah in front of John, he went into a rage and trashed his room. The rule was: any violent behavior and the inmate went back to the Kansas State Prison. And John went back.

Taking a Chance

I was working in my office late at night when a counselor from the state prison called and said John wanted to talk to me. John asked if he could come back, but I told him I would have to give it some serious thought. I knew the future of our program depended on not bringing anyone in who might act out violently.

I sat in my office that night with the lights turned off and prayed. I asked God to show me what to do. I believed that this program had so much to offer John, and I knew that this might be the last chance this 49-year-old man had to rid himself of the demonic thoughts and memories that he had held within for so long. The answer came: call the prison and ask them to bring John over to talk with me.

As he sat across from me in my office, I said: "John, there are two things you must agree to do before I even consider taking you back. One, you have to meet regularly with our psychologist." John said, "I will." "Second," I continued, "I cannot and will not tolerate any more violent behavior." "No more violence," he promised. Then this huge man started sobbing, saying, "No one has ever given me a second chance." Overnight John changed. It was a miracle.

He came back to KCIL, and from all appearances he was a different man. Now he smiled, laughed and talked with everyone. John served the next nine months as a model inmate, and after meeting with the parole board, he was expecting to be released.

Sadly, John died of a massive heart attack before he could be released. Yet I believe he did gain his freedom—freedom from whatever had hurt him in the past, freedom from the hurt he had caused, and freedom to be a person who enjoyed life to the fullest, right where he was.

Opening Doors

I believe my life could have taken a totally different turn, a wrong turn, if I hadn't received *Wee Wisdom* as a child. In the facilities where I served as director or warden, I witnessed how inmates' lives were often changed when Unity ministers brought *Daily Word* magazines and offered seminars that opened the door to a new life.

I think it's important that we reach out to people and let them know we care. Obviously, in helping people, we need to set some rules, just as I did with John. We can all open doors for others, but they must be willing to walk through them. We cannot take someone who has been deprived of everything, however, and say "Okay, here's the candy store." Change can be a slow process, but I believe everyone can move ahead with change—even one inch at a time.

I thank God for the opportunities I have had to make a difference in the lives of others. I thank God for the neighbor who sent me *Wee Wisdom*, for John, and for all the people who have made such a wonderful difference in my life.

Postscript

Sally Halford devoted more than 30 years to the field of corrections and served as director in county and state departments of correctional facilities throughout the Midwest. Her active career allowed her to be involved in truly innovative concepts such as private sector work for inmates and co-corrections. These new concepts allowed offenders to have opportunities to move beyond their original fate. Since officially retiring from the field of corrections, Sally continues to do consulting and expert witness testimony on occasion.

Sally and her husband live on a berry farm in northwest Missouri. "Most of my life today involves the daily activities associated with the small farm that my husband and I own," she says. "The blueberries seem to improve every year, both in abundance and quality. When I don't have my hand in other projects, I enjoy improving my skill at spinning fiber and knitting. I spin pet fur and mix different fibers for projects.

"Another passion is my love and concern for animals. We now have a family of three dogs (one with three legs), five house cats, plus one outside cat that has yet to be persuaded to come in out of the cold. Each of these family members either came from a shelter or was dropped off at our farm. One of these "dropees" had heartworms and hip dysplasia; today she is a healthy happy little dog. My life continues to evolve, and I enjoy each chapter as it unfolds."

41

TRUE NATURE

I am an ambassador of God's love!

My true nature is to express love and understanding toward others. This is the spirit of God within me, expressing as compassionate words and kind deeds.

Much of what I do in life may not seem significant, yet even with the simplest act, I am an ambassador of God. Knowing this, I expand my willingness to love and care. In my interactions, I choose kindness; in my thoughts, acceptance; in my heart, compassion.

Yes, I am kind and loving at home, at work, and in my community. And the spirit of God within me inspires me to love and to serve in even greater ways, making a difference in my world.

The fruit of the Spirit is love, joy, peace, patience, kindness, generosity, faithfulness, and gentleness, and self-control.
—Galatians 5:22-23

Preview

One of the benefits of my many years working at Unity Village was meeting and getting to know students who were going through ministerial training there. Some had given up lucrative careers, sold their homes, packed a few personal belongings to spend the next two to three years in classes at the Unity Institute. They came from near and far—from other states, countries and continents—to answer the call to become Unity ministers.

Besides spending hours attending classes, writing papers and studying, some students volunteered, once a week, to read the *Daily Word* message and pray with the employees of different departments of Unity. Those of us in the *Daily Word* editorial department were blessed by students who shared their time and also their faith with us on Thursdays—just before we would go to the 11 a.m. Silent Unity Healing Service. (Taking time to pray every day was another wonderful benefit of working at Unity.)

Randy Jones was assigned to the *Daily Word* department the year before I retired. Over the months, he became a trusted friend to all of us in the department. When he shared the story of what led him to ministerial school, we knew it was one that would also bless the *Daily Word* readers.

The Answer Is Love

By Randy Jones

The summer I turned 21, I started a job as a park ranger, and one of the first classes I took during training was a CPR course. A few weeks later another ranger and I were called to the scene of a drowning. We pulled a girl out of the water and began CPR. Amazingly, she began to breathe on her own. After helping a 16-year-old who was apparently dead come back to life, I was hooked on becoming a paramedic.

When I became a paramedic, however, questions came up about my belief in God. I felt as if the judgmental, harsh God I knew as a youth in church was passing judgment on me. Whenever I was unable to save a life, I thought it was my fault. After a while, I reached a point where I wondered if I could continue in this profession.

On a cold, snowy January day in Hutchinson, Kansas, my unit was called to help a woman who had slipped and fallen on her porch. It was a dreadful scene. The woman, who was in her 80s, had lain on her porch for about three hours before anyone noticed her.

When we paramedics arrived, she was actually frozen to the floor of the porch. A police officer who had put a cover over her body told us, "She's already dead." I put a monitor on her and found that she still had a heartbeat, although her heart rate was only 20 beats a minute. A normal heart rate is between 60 and 80.

While rushing her to the emergency room, we performed manual respiration on her, using a handheld squeeze bag. Once there, we slowly eased her into a bathtub of water to bring her body temperature back to normal. I was elated when she stirred and started breathing on her own.

On my very next call, however, I was devastated by what I faced. Earlier that night, two young parents had left their baby with a babysitter for the very first time. When they came home at midnight, their beautiful, perfect baby was dead. I felt *I* had lost that baby when I failed at resuscitating her. At that moment, I knew in my heart that I couldn't go on being a paramedic.

Over the course of the next few years, I attempted to change the direction of my career as I completed a bachelor's degree in finance and a master's in business. Still I was drawn back to helping people in crisis and became the manager of an emergency room.

Fruits of a Spiritual Journey

During this same time, I began a spiritual journey that led me to my Native American roots. This is where I put aside my belief in a judgmental God and accepted a God of love. I experienced what it was to be loved unconditionally by my Creator, just as I am. I learned to listen to that still small voice within and felt the oneness of creation.

I could not go back to the church of my youth, but I was searching for one that taught about a loving God and the oneness of all. I found this at the Unity Church of Wichita.

At Unity I was introduced to *Daily Word*, and it became my daily spiritual resource. I had become the administrator of a large cardiology group and was responsible for six locations and 13 outreach clinics. After stressful meetings in the morning where doctors would get into disagreements, I would go back to my desk and read the *Daily Word* message for that day. Each life-affirming, inspiring message was perfect for me. I started e-mailing messages to some of the people in our group. Then others asked me, "What's the word for the day?" and "May I have a copy of today's word?"

I saw that all of us who were reading *Daily Word* were letting our inner spiritual nature—the Christ spirit within—shine more brightly and become a part of how we treated one another and those we served. I realized the life-saving care we gave was important, but that the spiritual care we gave was even more important.

Connecting With the Christ Within

As a paramedic, I would sit by patients, talk to them and hold their hands, establishing a heart-to-heart relationship. I didn't know it then, but what I was doing was connecting the Christ in me with the Christ in them. I tried to be the best Christ that I could be and treat people accordingly. I believe this made a difference in the quality of their care and their recovery.

Later, as a manager, I understood that when I treated my employees with compassion and caring, that's how they would treat their patients. I reminded the doctors, "If you want your patients to have top-notch treatment, then you need to treat your employees that way."

The more we read *Daily Word*, the less sickness, anger and turmoil appeared in our group. As more and more people in our group related to one another and the patients from a Christ consciousness, the practice changed.

My compelling desire to be of service to others has led me to enroll in ministerial school to become a Unity minister. As a Unity minister, I want to share the truth about each and every one of us: We are free to be the Christ in expression toward others in our homes and our places of work. Living from the Christ love within our hearts, we are loving and caring toward others. We are one family of God, each one being loved unconditionally.

Postscript

After 30 years of service in the health-care industry, Randy Jones enrolled in the Master of Divinity program at Unity Institute. Randy and his wife, Charlotte, have two grown children, Joshua and Laura, and three granddaughters, Anita, Aliyyah and Nina. Randy was able to be there for the births of both Aliyyah and Nina and says, "No matter what other title I may earn, 'grandparent' will remain my favorite."

"Our decision to answer the call to ministry has been an incredible blessing for Charlotte and me. We understand that our life is not about rushing around *doing* good here and there; it's about *being* that good in every circumstance and in every moment. With this change in focus, we see the Christ in ourselves, in all people and in all of Creation."

42

JOY

My soul sings a song of joy.

Many different activities connect me to the joy that is deep within me. Being enveloped by the silence of a snowfall may fill me with quiet joy. Listening to a choir or joining in the singing of my favorite songs may lift my spirits.

The simple touch of a loved one's hand or the gentle support of a caregiver may lighten my heart. Lighting a candle, saying a prayer and blessing a meal can all be sources of joy in my day.

Whatever the activity, I realize joy when my mind is fixed on finding Spirit within each of my experiences. True and lasting joy comes from within—from God, the Source of every joy.

Clap your hands, all you peoples; shout to God with loud songs of joy.—Psalm 47:1

Preview

Although the only music I play is on my iPod and the only time I sing is while alone, I have witnessed the joy of others who sing and play musical instruments. My father was a fiddle player from

Arkansas, and some of my earliest memories are of listening to him play. One of my favorites was the beautiful haunting melody of "Wednesday Night Waltz." As I listened, I would picture myself in a ball gown, being guided across the floor by a handsome prince. When my father sang gospel songs, his face lit up in a joy that I knew had transported him. He was physically there but his spirit was soaring.

Music planted seeds of faith in Cheryl Farrell's heart when she was a young girl. Faith grew within her over the years, providing her spiritual understanding that brought her through challenging times.

Making a Joyful Noise

By Cheryl Farrell

Music has infused every stage of my life with meaning. I started singing in church when I was about 7 years old. I have sung in school programs, at weddings and memorial services, and as a part of my job as a member of the "Clue Crew" on the television quiz show *Jeopardy!*

Gospel music, in particular, has been with me all along. I find that when I am going through a challenging time, the lyrics of a hymn come to mind. It's as if the lyrics are part of the vocabulary God uses to speak to me. Decades later, the songs I learned as an antsy child sitting in church on Sunday mornings are a reservoir of faith-filled messages within me.

A Dream Comes True

Since childhood, my dream had been to marry and have children. Wendell and I were both 29 when we married. Unfortunately, my chronic abdominal pain proved to be a severe case of endometriosis, a common cause of infertility. One doctor recommended that I have a hysterectomy, but I wouldn't accept not being able to have children. After consulting another physician, I had corrective surgery; yet it was six more years before I became pregnant.

Because of the surgery and my age, my pregnancy was termed "high risk." The doctor strongly recommended I have a delivery by Cesarean section. My pregnancy took a major turn during the seventh month when I suddenly began to hemorrhage.

A heavy rain that had begun earlier that day continued and even intensified. Wendell worked two hours away, so I called for an ambulance. As I was rushed to a hospital, I heard concern in the voices of the EMTs as they checked my vitals. My blood pressure was dangerously low. I knew that both the lives of my baby and myself were in peril. I lay on the gurney, shivering and questioning, God, why is this happening? My baby and I have come so far to have the pregnancy end now.

Once in the operating room—as if in answer to prayer—verses from the hymns of my childhood began to play in my mind, taking on fresh, new meaning for me. "We've Come This Far by Faith" reminded me that I had been through trying times before, and God had seen me through. Then another hymn came to me: "Lead Me, Guide Me." I felt no fear. I knew I was on a divinely led path.

While I'll concede that it might have been the anesthesia, an amazing wash of peace settled over me. I went into surgery hearing a musical message of hope and faith. I knew everything was going to be all right.

I felt a joy for life that I had never before experienced for the wonderful gift of my son. Alec was born weighing 3 pounds and 15 ounces. He was in neonatal intensive care at the hospital for his first six weeks. The day we finally took him home was a jubilee!

Alec's early years were typical: filled with bedtime prayers, playtimes, visits from the tooth fairy, scraped knees and school. One of my favorite memories of him was when he was in kindergarten. At that time, he was learning about the human body—the names and sizes of internal organs. One afternoon, I was in a particularly cuddly mood. I approached Alec with my arms wide open, saying, "Honey, I love you this much." I then asked him, "How much do you love me?"

He pondered my question and then raised one small hand to show the distance (about three inches) between his thumb and forefinger. "Oh, don't you love me as much as I love you?" I questioned.

Continuing to hold out his hand with his thumb and forefinger extended, Alec looked up and said, "Mommy, that's the size of my heart!"

I've been told there is not a correlation with my son's premature birth and his being diagnosed with type 1 diabetes at age 10. I didn't know much about juvenile diabetes then. Like other times in my life, I found myself asking, God, what would you have me do? What came to mind was that I was to take whatever gifts, resources, interests and assets I had and bring them to bear in doing God's work.

Part of that work was to do something to help the Juvenile Diabetes Research Foundation International (JDRF).

Two award-winning composers had written a song for JDRF called "Promise to Remember Me"—a powerful call to lawmakers to understand the struggles of children who live with diabetes. I received permission to record the song with proceeds from the sales going to JDRF.

A Bright Light

Alec is a teenager now—a strapping 160-pound, avid lacrosse player. He has a lovely spirit, a bright light. I say that he was my little acorn that has grown into a huge oak tree! We continue to pray for a cure, and he does well in overcoming the challenge of managing this disease. Wendell and I have tried to teach him and his younger sister Nia that we all have the strength and faith to take whatever we are given in life and make something good from it. There's a blessing that comes from the challenges.

As always, those Sunday school songs come back to me with new meaning, speaking directly to my heart. "Make a Joyful Noise." Give God the glory in all situations. My favorite verse in Scripture, Matthew 5:16, says: "In the same way, let your light shine before others, so that they may see your good works and give glory to your Father in heaven."

And that's what I try to do as I let God's spirit work through me.

Postscript

Cheryl Farrell lives in California with her husband Wendell, son Alec, and daughter Nia Grace. For more information about her "Promise to Remember Me" recording, visit *www.bayheartmusic.com*. For information about the Juvenile Diabetes Research Foundation, log on to *www.jdrf.org*.

As a professional singer, Cheryl is dedicated to sharing musical messages of hope for the important cause of diabetes research. She cherishes her musical "adventures" in her former role as a clue-giver on the television quiz show *Jeopardy!*

Cheryl has written about families facing the challenges of living with type 1 diabetes. She has appeared on news programs and met with audiences, describing the constant work of managing blood sugar levels, which is especially important for young people who are most often stricken with the disease. "My mission," she says, "is to help find a cure for diabetes."

43

WORDS OF TRUTH

I boldly and gratefully accept the gifts of Spirit.

An affirmation is not merely wishful thinking; it is a statement of truth by which I claim the good that is mine to claim. With positive affirmations, I boldly and gratefully accept the gifts of Spirit.

Conditions in the outer adjust to agree with God's bountiful provision, and I am uplifted to a better understanding of my unity with my Creator. This clears the way for divine perfection to be revealed.

God breathes through me as the inspiration for positive, life-affirming words—words of health and wholeness, of abundance and infinite supply, of thanksgiving for blessings, both seen and unseen. Words of truth confirm all that God provides.

Let the words of my mouth and the meditation of my heart be
acceptable to you, O Lord, my rock and my redeemer.
—Psalm 19:14

Preview

When in a crowd at an airport or some event, I look around at the people there and wonder what the stories of their lives might be and how many are *Daily Word* readers. I'm never surprised when I learn that *Daily Word* is important in the life of someone—whether the person is a neighbor, a new acquaintance or a well-known celebrity.

More than 20 years ago, I was taking a college course in the arts and humanities. In addition to my full-time employment at Unity, I attended classes one night a week and for a weekend once a month. At 5 a.m. every weekday morning, I watched a TV course that Dr. Maya Angelou hosted. She held my undivided attention even at this early hour. As I watched and listened, I felt as if Dr. Angelou took me by the hand and led through a history of art, dance and theater. With her gentle, melodious voice, she described the tempo of music, scenes of theatrical productions and brush strokes of works of art that brought them to life in my imagination.

I didn't know until years later in conversation with her niece Rosa Johnson that *Daily Word* was a part of Dr. Angelou's experience every day. Rosa is indeed her aunt's niece. Learning of Rosa's strength, faith and love of family, I gave thanks that she is someone who reads and applies the same *Daily Word* message of inspiration in life that I and millions of others do every day. Along with Rosa and Dr. Angelou, there is a *Daily Word* network of like-minded spiritual seekers who contribute to the well-being of our world.

The Power of the Word

By Rosa Johnson

At age 14, I was going through the challenges that most teenagers typically go through. Then my aunt, Dr. Maya Angelou, introduced me to *Daily Word*. She taught me to know that, despite negative appearances, God is all there is. Knowing this and having *Daily Word* saved me from taking missteps that many teenagers are apt to take.

As the daughter of her brother Bailey, whom she has written about in her books, I am Aunt Maya's only niece, and she is my only aunt. She and I have a very close and loving relationship.

When I was a child, she instilled in me the truth of the oneness of all people. She took me to several churches in San Francisco where she lived. On many occasions we attended the Christian Science church and the Unity church there.

I have three grown children, and all of them read *Daily Word*—as do their children. Four generations of our family are currently reading it. We give *Daily Word* as Christmas and birthday gifts. Often the guests in our homes find a current copy on their bedside tables. It has been a tool for our upliftment and encouragement during times of flagging faith, joyous celebration and tremendous loss.

In every *Daily Word*, the reader is given an invitation to call or write the Silent Unity prayer ministry. Thirteen years ago I lost a son to HIV—a very traumatic experience for me. While he was sick and prior to his passing, I requested the prayer support of Silent Unity many times. I am so thankful for Silent Unity and its prayer network of people all over the world.

I live about a 10-minute drive from Aunt Maya. She believes our lives are extended by several years when someone who loves us is living within a 10-mile radius of where we live. When she is traveling, whatever city or state she happens to be in, I call her and read the word for the day to her.

Perfect Fit

No matter what the message for the day is, it fits with something that is happening in my life or in the life of someone I know. I have e-mailed and faxed *Daily Word* messages to friends and family all over the world. I have copies of *Unity Magazine*® and *Daily Word* that I have saved, and I share them with friends and family near and far. This is a good way to keep in touch with those I love and to stay in touch with Spirit.

I am Aunt Maya's archivist, event planner, and conservationist of her art collection, which includes an extensive outdoor sculpture garden. When she noticed that the swimming pool near the garden wasn't being used, Aunt Maya decided it needed to be filled in and a dance floor built over it.

After obtaining the licenses for the project, I located a carpenter who offered a wonderful design for the dance floor. One day as he was leaving, he said, "Wait a minute, Ms. Johnson. Let me give you something." I said okay, and he handed me a page from *Daily Word*. I believe Spirit led him to do this. When I told Aunt Maya, she said, "Oh, yes! He's our man!"

You never know where or when *Daily Word* will turn up, and I am thankful for all in the Unity family. The magazine gives me hope. As a human being, I am subject to the ups and downs of life, but when I start my morning with *Daily Word*, I set my course for the day—a very elevated course.

The power contained in words cannot be minimized. Words can be the healing tools of the Divine. Used in conjunction with abiding faith, words can heal and uplift individuals and all of humanity.

Postscript

Rosa Johnson is co-author of *Maya Angelou: A Glorious Celebration*, published by Doubleday.

As an update to her story in *Daily Word*, Rosa Johnson says, "My life is so full that I didn't know where to start. My family was overjoyed to see my thoughts published in such an important magazine as *Daily Word*. My aunt, Dr. Maya Angelou, requested that she receive over 50 copies of that issue, which she promptly mailed to her friends near and far. When Oprah Winfrey read it, she, too, was impressed with the honest telling of my story.

"There has been great sadness also. In the act of fleeing an abusive relationship, my 25-year-old granddaughter LaTasha and her 2-year-old son Amir relocated to Puerto Rico. Amir had an aggressive form of cancer that started in his left eye, which was removed prior to the move to Puerto Rico.

"When I was told that the cancer had moved to Amir's brain and possibly to his spine, by the grace of God, I remained focused enough to arrange a flight to San Juan, Puerto Rico. From the moment I decided to travel, my mind was geared toward packing whatever would be needed in a tropical environment, along with reading material that would assist me in being the spirit-driven grandmother that La Tasha and Amir would need. I took my current *Daily Word* along with other uplifting soul-inspiring texts.

"While there, *Daily Word* was my constant companion, support structure and saving grace. Since Amir's passing, I have more than ever turned to *Daily Word* as a source of comfort and encouragement during this incredible time of loss.

"During the time they were in Puerto Rico, LaTasha was able to totally focus on her loving relationship with Amir. The people of their community were soon caught up in the aura of total trust and embracing dedication to her son's well-being that LaTasha exhibited. It was as if this loving little boy truly belonged to everyone who came in contact with him.

_44_

GOD'S PRESENCE

In every moment, I live and move in the presence of God.

When I remember that this is God's beautifully created world, I realize that there is nothing in the entire world to fear.

There is no place on earth where God's presence is not. My mind and heart are at peace knowing that wherever I go, I am in the midst of God's love and goodness.

God is love. People and all creation give expression to the goodness of God as beauty, love, kindness and so much more.

I live and move and have my very existence in the presence of good. I am awake to and aware of God's presence. In the realization that God's love and goodness surround me, I am fearless.

If I forget and get caught up in the world and its fears, the "still small voice" of God speaks to me, calms me and puts me at ease. I am at peace again.

Let not your hearts be troubled, neither let them be afraid.
—John 14:27

Preview

Sometimes learning what others have experienced in life is difficult. Listening and reading about others who have gone through dark passages on their journeys of life, we are hoping for a happy ending. Yet life itself is about new beginnings every day and every moment. We never have to become stuck in fear or remorse when we go to Spirit within for the wisdom, the strength, the courage to go through those dark passages.

Within each of us there is an inner light, a sacred presence that is always present and ready to guide us. Rhonda Britten's story is one that bears witness to this truth.

From Fear to Faith

By Rhonda Britten

I was a 14-year-old planning on being a minister when my father and mother decided to divorce. Even in this time of uncertainty, I felt as if God and I were one—we were buddies. I had started a youth group at my church, went to teen summits and handed out "God leaflets" everywhere.

Several months after Dad had moved out of our house, he came over to take my mother, my two sisters—Cindy and Linda—and me to a Father's Day brunch.

That day started off just like most other days—my sisters and I arguing about whose turn it was to be in the bathroom. My mother was in her bedroom putting on her blue eye shadow and puffing up her beehive hairdo when my father arrived. He mumbled something to me about him going to get his coat from the car. I went to Mom's room to tell her Dad was here and we were ready to go.

Just as Mom and I walked to the car, Dad pulled out a gun. He yelled at my mother, "You made me do this!" and shot her.

"Stop, stop, stop!" I yelled. "I'll live with you! I'll take care of you!" I was trying to say anything to make him stop shooting.

Then he pointed the gun at me, and we stared at each other for a few seconds. He blinked, cocked the gun, turned toward Mom, and shot her a second time. Dad came running over to me, got down on his knees, put the gun to his head and fired.

As the witness to my father murdering my mother and taking his own life, I was haunted by the violence and the loss of two people I loved. But I also felt as if somehow their deaths were my fault. Dad killed Mom because he loved her and couldn't live without her. I apparently was not worth living for because my offering to live with Dad and take care of him didn't stop him. So I rationalized that I wasn't worth living for or even worth killing.

I believed God was testing me on June 15, 1975, the day my parents died. I drew a line in the sand between God and me, saying: "I love You; I just can't give You my life like I said I would. I've got to take it back because Your tests are too hard. It's too hard to love You."

Staying Alive

My older sister Cindy was 18, so my younger sister Linda and I lived with her. I did not drink or smoke at the time, and I got straight As in school. By the time I turned 16, I was able to move into my own apartment with the money I made as a waitress and with my monthly Social Security survivor's benefit checks.

Every night I had nightmares in which my father chased me and shot at me. Over the years I used alcohol to numb myself so I could fall asleep. It wasn't until my third suicide attempt at age 25 that I accepted that I must be staying alive for a purpose. I knew I needed to figure out another way to live my life, because I couldn't keep doing what I was doing.

I made the choice to quit blaming my parents for the life I had and to start looking at my own worthiness. I bought a big calendar and some stick-on stars from the office supply store. Each day that I did something I considered good, I put a star on the calendar. After a month, I realized I did a lot of good and I was not a bad person. With this simple exercise and by taking responsibility for my life, I began on a path of what I now call "Fearless Living."

I quit drinking and started going to church again. I prayed but I couldn't say the name "God." Then one day as I was coming home from church, I heard God's voice, which I had not listened to for more than 20 years. For whatever reason, that day God came through to me and said, "I need you." "Forget it," I said. "You cost too much. What do I have to sacrifice in order for You to love me?"

I had to pull the car over because I was literally having a dialogue with God. I wanted to have a relationship with God, and yet I felt that crossing the line back to God meant something bad would happen. I must have sat on the side of the road for two hours, crying and talking.

Eventually I said, "Okay, God, I do want the connection with You that I had at 14—more than anything else." The happiest I had ever been was right before my parents died, when I had a relationship with God.

In my car on that day, I realized I was living in fear that if I was happy in a relationship with God again, someone else would die. I was able to push past that fear and cry out, "God, I can no longer deny You!"

In that moment I surrendered and gave my life back to God. I'm pleased to say nobody died! I started a daily dialogue with God again in prayer and communion, and wonderful ideas for fearless living kept coming to me.

Living Without Fear

People started noticing a positive difference in me and asked, "How did you change your life?" I told them about my first exercise using the calendar and other exercises I had tried with success, and they came back and said: "Wow, that really helped me too. What else do you have?" The floodgate opened, and within months I started realizing that my purpose was to live my life without fear and to help others do the same.

We can find ourselves serving fear rather than God when we are so afraid of making mistakes that we do nothing but wait for God to give us an answer to our purpose in life. God may have already given us guidance on that, but out of fear, we did not take the responsibility of following it. Then we spend our lives believing we are patiently waiting for something when God has already given it to us.

Listening to God

With spiritual understanding, I have learned to distinguish when God is talking to me and when fear is talking to me. Able to distinguish between those voices, I'm willing to listen to God and to take responsibility in following God's guidance.

I believe in the 24-hour, seven-days-a-week prayer. I advocate a continuous connection with God in the sense that I literally am praying all the time. First thing in the morning, I listen to spiritual music that connects me to God. Anytime I become upset, to again connect with God, I ask myself: "I'm willing to see this differently. Where is God at work here?"

For years I would ask, "What's wrong with me?" I never focused on what was right about me. When I surrendered my life back to God, I realized I had been asking the wrong questions for the last 20 years. The fact is, there's nothing wrong with me. There's nothing wrong with any of us. The question is, "What are we afraid of?" Is it fear of failure, of intimacy, or of being alone? Once we are clear that fear is not going to run our lives, God can use us fully.

Only then are we being true to the way God created us to be. Fear thrives on the false belief that doing nothing keeps us safe. In reality, we thrive when we take risks, God's risks. When God's voice becomes our main motivator, fear will no longer be in the forefront. We will no longer be afraid to reach out, ask for help, and follow our passion. We will, finally, stay true to our essential nature and be at peace.

Postscript

Rhonda Britten, Emmy Award-winner and repeat guest of *The Oprah Winfrey Show*, is the Life Coach on the highly successful VH1 reality show *Celebrity Fit Club* and founder of the Fearless Living Institute (*www.FearlessLiving.org*), an organization dedicated to giving everyone the tools they need to master their emotional fears.

During her three seasons on the hit daytime reality drama *Starting Over*, Rhonda was named "America's Favorite Life Coach" and was dubbed *Starting Over*'s "Most Valuable Player" by *The New York Times*. She is a globally recognized expert on the subject of fear and fearlessness. Her books include *Fearless Living* (translated into 12 languages), *Fearless Loving*, *Change Your Life in 30 Days* and *Do I Look Fat in This? Get Over Your Body and On With Your Life.*

45

LIFE OF PRAYER

I continue steadfastly in prayer and grow in spiritual understanding.

What relation has prayer to successful living? Prayer is the lifting of thoughts to God; prayer is the seeking for more light and more understanding. Prayer is the deepening and the expanding of innate faith. Prayer is the quickening of Spirit within.

To seek to know myself as spiritual being is to awaken in myself greater capacity for living and giving. To bring my thoughts and feelings to the loving Christ is to make myself a more productive channel. To stir up the God qualities within me is to make myself more vitally alive. What relation has prayer to successful living? It has a direct relation, a direct bearing. If I feel that my life could be different and that I could give more or be more, I begin with prayer. The more I increase my awareness of the abundant Spirit of God within, the more richly I am blessed in everything I do and the more successful I am in meeting the experiences of life.

Continue steadfastly in prayer.—Colossians 4:2

Preview

When I discovered Unity, I knew I was coming home to teachings, to an affirmative way of life, to a community that would support and encourage me no matter what challenge or opportunity was before me.

I've learned what to expect when I attend a Silent Unity or Unity Village Chapel service at the Village or a Unity church service elsewhere: principles and teachings of Truth based on the power and presence of God in all and through all. Not that I am partial, but I believe that Unity people are some of the warmest, welcoming people I have ever met.

Sharon Connors had been the minister at the Unity Village Chapel, which is located on the Unity Village campus, for only a short time when I first attended one of her services. I was relaxed and ready for the usual order of service. First on the agenda, however, was a request by Rev. Connors; she asked all of us in the Chapel to greet our neighbors. She stepped away from the lectern and took part in the welcoming. I greeted the person on either side of me, and the next moment, I was sitting alone. My neighbors had moved on to greet others. Rev. Connors' enthusiasm was contagious, and I was soon joining with the stream of people who were moving up and down the aisles. As I looked around at the people in the chapel that day, I was reminded of a greeting I had heard many times in Unity: The Christ in me greets the Christ in you.

A New Kind of Prayer Life

By Rev. Sharon Connors

In the late 70s, I felt as if my life was falling apart, and I did not know where to turn. A friend told me she was sending me something she felt would help. That something was *Daily Word* magazine. I hung on to its every word, and it brought me hope.

Some years passed, and I was working in a friend's boutique. My life again had taken a downward turn: my marriage was on the rocks, and my two teenage children were in trouble every time I turned around. One evening my friend came into the showroom of the boutique as I was closing. Taking one look at me, she asked, "How are things?"

When I started to cry, she said, "I know what we're going to do." She walked me back into her office and pulled a phone number out of her purse. "I'm going to call Silent Unity and then hand the phone to you. You'll hear a voice, but don't worry about what to say. Just speak from your heart."

I listened and heard a soothing voice: "Hello, this is Silent Unity. How may we pray with you?" I can't remember what I said, but when I hung up that phone, something had shifted in me. Hopelessness and confusion were replaced by a sense of peace. A huge burden had been lifted.

That was just the beginning of a new kind of prayer life for me. In 1982 a friend took me to a Unity church. Unity offered me a different kind of God than the punishing and whimsical one I had learned about in the faith of my early years. I now had the understanding that God is all good, all loving, and always the same dependable God. I was taught to pray from a consciousness that I was made of this all-good, unconditionally loving and infallibly wise energy.

When I started going to the Unity church, I took every class that was offered. One bright Sunday afternoon, I was sitting in a dynamic workshop at church when an inner voice said, "This is what you are to do." No way! I thought. This would cause way too much trouble in my life. I finally listened to that voice, however, and entered Unity's ministerial school in 1985.

One of my first assignments was to pick a healing project for the quarter. The instructor challenged the students to pray and meditate, visualizing a healing of the condition. I had a chronic infection that I began to pray about—affirming a healing and visualizing myself filled with healing light. I gave thanks in advance. At the end of the quarter, the infection was gone!

A couple of years into my ministry, however, I was having some alarming symptoms and was given an MRI, which revealed a tumor on my pituitary gland.

Rather casually the doctor said: "We don't want to do brain surgery on you. There is medication that will inhibit the growth of the tumor. That's the best we can do. The tumor will continue to grow if you don't take this medicine."

I tried the medicine, but it made me sicker. I decided to stop taking it and to pray with a real intentional focus of visualizing and affirming that the tumor was gone, just as I had done with the infection. Seeing a healing light in my head and visualizing the tumor dissolving, I gave thanks that it was gone. Two MRIs later, the tumor was gone.

It's good for the soul and for the expansion and deepening of our faith to take time to reflect on the incredible ways that prayer changes things. There has never been a time when I prayed that I didn't feel better. My prayers aren't about me changing God; they are helping me experience more of God.

Prayer has become central to my life. I have joked that my children drove me to the ministry because they kept me praying and seeking God's guidance. Prayer got me through times of challenge with my children, and today they are doing really well. I am a witness for parents who feel as though they are going to lose their minds if their kids don't change. I tell concerned parents, "There really is hope. Just keep praying."

Prayer is central to my ministry also. The church staff prays every morning and at every staff meeting before and after. We have a prayer team at the church that is there to pray after every service with congregants who want prayer support. I've never seen it fail; whenever we join in prayer, there's a shift in the energy. People's faces brighten into smiles, and there is an increase of vitality.

Prayer is the language of spirituality. And if we want to have a relationship with God that is dynamic and organic and nourishing, we have to invest ourselves in it just as we would in any healthy relationship. Prayer is that investment—and there's always a return on that investment.

Ever since I began to start and end my day with prayer, my days are brighter and my life is better. I believe praying affirmatively is more effective than praying from fear. Our desire to make a connection with the Divine creates the connection, and something good *does* happen.

It doesn't matter what the challenge is. Prayer helps. It connects our minds with Divine Mind, opening the way to receive the resources of heaven.

Postscript

Ordained in 1988, Rev. Sharon Connors holds a master's degree in counseling from Northeastern Illinois University. She currently serves as senior minister at Christ Church Unity in El Cajon, California. Prior to her move to California, she served as senior minister at Unity Village Chapel at Unity World Headquarters. Sharon has also served ministries in Clearwater and Gainesville, Florida, and in San Francisco, California.

Along with her full-time ministry, Sharon serves in various capacities: chairperson of the Board of Trustees for the Association of Unity Churches International; the advisory council for the Association for Global New Thought; board of directors for Bread for the Journey; board of directors for Holos Graduate Theological Seminary; and on the editorial board of *Unity Magazine*.

She is the author of *Adventures in Prayer: Praying Your Way to a God You Can Trust*, published by Bantam. Her writing has appeared in *Guideposts*, *Spirituality & Health*, *Unity Magazine* and *Daily Word*.

Sharon continues to practice what she "preaches," saying: "The more you experiment with willingness for God's will to be done, however unknown or inscrutable it may be in the moment of prayer, the more you will come to experience the brilliance of God's divine plan for your life."

46

BLESS THE CHILDREN

God bless children, for they are the teachers and peacemakers of the world.

When I contemplate the miracles of life and the hope that children are, I realize that they find joy in so many things that adults have forgotten. Children remind grown-ups how to be pure joy in expression.

To be in the presence of children is to look through the eyes of those who live each day to the fullest, who perceive a miracle in every situation. Children are life's greatest teachers, for to them, all people are beautiful, all ability levels are special, and all cultures and backgrounds are marvelous and interesting.

I take the time to mentor and care for the children, even as they mentor and care about me. The children in my life are well fed, well cared for and always have someone to look up to and trust.

Jesus said, "Let the little children come to me, and do not stop them; for it is to such as these that the kingdom of heaven belongs."—Matthew 19:14

Preview

One of the highest calls we can answer in life is to nurture children. Whether they are living in our own homes or elsewhere in the world, there are ways that we can assure that children have opportunities to grow into healthy, whole adults.

God has endowed all children with unlimited potential. Our role as family, friends and mentors is not to shape children by arranging their lives the way we want them to be. Instead, we are to provide them with a safe, diverse environment in which to learn and grow. This means there are times we step forward to help them get through a challenge and also times we step aside so that they gain self-confidence in doing for themselves.

We may never know how much help our giving financial assistance or offering an encouraging word may be. However, the still small voice within us is our constant guide in knowing how to enrich the lives of children and to also know that as we do we also enrich our own lives as well.

In childhood, Stacy Maciuk seemed to have little chance to survive, to lead a healthy, whole life as an adult. Yet, as she listened to that still small voice within, she not only survived, she flourished. Stacy has ensured that other children are protected and nurtured so that they have opportunities to express their God-given potential. She has answered that call to nurture children in abundant ways.

God Has Carried Me Through

By Stacy Maciuk

By the grace of God, I don't have many memories of being abused as a child. Between the ages of 2 and 9, I had been taken away from, and given back to, my birth mother several times and then placed in several different foster homes in Tennessee. At age 9, also by the grace of God, I was placed in the home of a devoted, caring foster mother whom I call Mom.

Mom, a true unsung hero, has cared for foster children for more than two decades now. I can't remember how many kids came through her home—several before me and after. She still cares for two mentally-challenged adults she took in 20 years ago as foster kids. If not for her, they would be in a mental institution. Mom is a very special person who has opened her heart and her life to accept foster children—several with special needs.

When I moved to Nashville to live with Mom, I didn't have religion forced on me. I was allowed to go to several churches and choose the one I wanted to attend. I felt as if God kept bringing me back to Christ Church of Nashville. Prayer, the Bible and fellowship have been so important to my spiritual growth.

My life has been so good since I became part of Mom's family. Before then, however, I lived in several abusive homes and was acting out at school. Everybody believed I was the problem. To fix my behavior problems, I was given medications and placed in special education classes from grades three to five. No one understood that the real problem was the abuse that I was going through where I lived.

Today, we tend to look at children in the context of their environment, but this certainly was not the case then. Mom believed in me, and she had friends who also took an interest in me. Mom worked for a doctor, and he and his wife made it possible for me to attend private schools from sixth grade through college, undergraduate and graduate schools. I didn't look at this as a free ride, however. Instead, I made an investment in my education, studying and being tutored every free moment I had.

A Call to Action

I attended Belmont University in Nashville for my undergraduate studies. During my sophomore year, I was asked to be on the Tennessee Youth Advisory Council that was just being formed. It is a part of the Jim Casey Youth Opportunities Initiative, a national initiative that focuses on improving outcomes for youth who are aging out of foster care.

Learning more about how other children were struggling to simply survive in the foster care system was a call to action for me. I learned that when most foster kids move, they carry their few belongings in a plastic trash bag. While serving on the council, my first initiative was a suitcase drive. More than 2,000 pieces of luggage were collected for youths in foster care. The suitcase drive was so successful that child advocacy centers across the entire state of Tennessee continue to collect suitcases for the children in care.

My next initiative was to draft a tuition waiver bill for the state of Tennessee. The theory behind the bill was that if the state invested up front to educate youths, it would not have to support them later as adults—possibly incarcerated, on welfare, or turning their own children over to foster care. Foster kids are 30 times more likely to be incarcerated and 30 times less likely to receive bachelor degrees than other children. But with an education, they can find good jobs and become tax-paying citizens of our society.

After two years of our educating and lobbying the state assembly, I saw the bill passed in the form of the governor's scholarship. Now youths in foster care in Tennessee have their tuition and other expenses waived for all four years at any state university.

Supporting Our Kids

One of the most incredible honors in my life was being a speaker at my own college graduation—a foster kid who, through the help of generous people, was graduating. The president of Belmont, Dr. Bob Fisher, wrote me a note of congratulations. I wrote him back, thanked him, and asked for his support of young people in foster care. He agreed and set up a committee to help. Today, there is a $2.5 million endowed scholarship at Belmont University for foster kids' use!

Generally when foster children turn 18, they age out of care and are sent out in the world on their own. As a member of Mom's family, I received continued support—spiritually, emotionally, and physically.

Sadly, I do have a brother who did not. When parents lose custody, their children are often placed separately. My brother spent most of his childhood in a group home. When he was 15, Mom took him in, but he was unable to make the transition and ended up in prison.

I pray every single day for children that are entering foster care. Just in my county alone, there are thousands of youths in the system. I pray that siblings will be placed together in one foster home with caring adults who help them build self-esteem. I pray that more singles and couples become foster parents. We have a national crisis concerning foster children, because there are not enough families for them.

I believe we can all take responsibility for helping foster kids, even if it's doing something little, because something we think is little can be huge for these kids. Congregations can become involved—first, by keeping these children in their prayers; then, by taking foster kids under their wings, making sure they know there are people who care about them. Individuals can send a foster child a note saying, "I've been praying for you, and I know God has good things in store for you."

When we share stories of the successes of foster kids, we replace messages of negativity with messages of hope. God is so good. In my situation, there were many different ways my life could have gone; but, like in the poem "Footprints," I believe God carried me along the right path.

Postscript

Stacy and her husband James Maciuk own a consulting and contracting company, EcoBuild of TN, LLC (*www.ecobuildtn.com*), which is focused on the construction and retrofit of low-impact homes. Stacy also works at Belmont University in Nashville as the associate director of Donor Relations.

Through her dedication, ingenuity and advocacy, Stacy has changed the lives of children in the foster care system in her community and beyond. She started the Tennessee Chapter of the Foster Care Alumni of America (FCAA). In addition to raising money for scholarships at Belmont, she also raises money for the foster care program, which includes scholarships, recruitment and other programs for retention (including books on loan and a free meal plan).

Since Stacy's story appeared in *Daily Word*, the Maciuks have added a member to their young family: their daughter Savannah Marie. Although Stacy is busy being a mother now, she still devotes time to her passion of helping foster kids. She says that a woman who had read her article in *Daily Word* connected her with a couple of sources for providing clothes for foster kids. "One is an annual consignment sale of high-end clothes that belonged to kids who attend private schools," she says. "After the sale this year, the parents who organized the sale allowed me to pick out clothes for foster kids at a very reasonable price. I didn't come to the sale prepared, taking only one other person with me. Next spring, I will be sure to have more help in selecting the clothes and in transporting them from the sale."

To learn more about foster care, visit *www.fostercaremonth.org*.

47

SPIRITUALLY CENTERED

Spiritually centered, I follow through on a divine plan.

I may feel complete in heart and mind as I reflect upon my past. However, Spirit within encourages me to look forward.

Spiritually centered, I do not base my expectations upon the past—what happened, who I was with, what I did or said. Memories can provide inspiration or insight, but I do not allow them to restrict me.

In prayerful meditation, I receive new revelations of divine inspiration. I see past old limitations. I recognize that I have resources, strength and insight. My comprehension expands beyond what I would have usually considered.

Infused with new ideas and energy, I am spiritually centered. Aligned with Spirit, I follow through on a divine plan.

I am about to do a new thing; now it springs forth, do you not perceive it?—Isaiah 43:19

Preview

My conversation with Dr. Wayne Dyer about a feature story in *Daily Word* was over the phone. I remember thinking I should get to the point and not take any more of this world-renowned author and speaker's time than necessary. A few moments into our conversation, however, he asked if I would mind waiting while he answered a call from one of his daughters. He was traveling and had been away from home for several weeks.

Of course I was more than willing to wait. I expected to be put on hold but realized he had placed the receiver down and was talking on another phone. I couldn't help from hearing him say the Midwest state he was presently in. When he came back on the line, he told me he always asked his children the capital of the state he was in on that particular day of his travels. I can't remember if he said she had given him the right answer, but I believe he was so right for taking that call. I admired him more than ever for being a father who took the time to stay in touch with his children.

A Spiritual Solution

By Dr. Wayne Dyer

I was 19 years old and in the Navy aboard a ship in the Pacific, reading the book *The Death of Ivan Ilyich* by Leo Tolstoy. Ivan Ilyich was a civil servant who every day went back and forth and did the job that he had been programmed to do. Although he felt that he had a greater calling, a greater mission, he never had the courage to abandon the kinds of things that he was doing and pursue his mission. At the end of the novel, as Ivan is lying on his deathbed and looking up at his wife, he questions whether his whole life has been wrong. Then he dies.

As soon as I finished the book, I wrote a note to myself: "Dear Wayne, don't die with your music still in you." And what I wrote on that day at the age of 19 became one of my 10 secrets for success and inner peace that I now share with millions of people as a writer and lecturer.

All of the secrets for success and inner peace are ideas that I have been accumulating since I was a young boy. Over the years I have been speaking to audiences in Unity churches and other venues throughout the world about these ten principles, and I am raising my children according to them.

The producers of national public television were interested in doing a series on two of my books, but they were a bit skeptical that a message about spirituality, higher consciousness, love, kindness and joy—so many of the things that Unity is all about—would be an incentive for viewers to send in pledge dollars.

However, after numerous nationwide broadcasts of television specials on *10 Secrets for Success and Inner Peace* and *There Is a Spiritual Solution to Every Problem*, over $36 million has been raised for public television.

This was confirmation of the tremendous receptivity people have to the ideas of improving the quality of their lives by making a closer connection to God and to one another. It's nice that what I am doing through these shows is raising money for public television, but my real mission is to raise the consciousness of the world.

Each of the 10 secrets or ideas helps people have a deeper, richer sense of being connected to God and to everyone. This is one thing that people are confronted with in our society today. They feel disconnected from others even though here on planet Earth, we all breathe the same air, are warmed by the same sun, drink the same water and have the same rain fall on us.

We don't share the same ideas about who we are and what we are doing because we feel so disconnected from one another. One of my missions is to help all people around the world feel more connected. I illustrate this in an update of an old story I tell in my lectures:

A grandfather is talking to his grandson a few days after the terrorist attacks of 9/11. Looking at his grandson, the grandfather says: "I feel like I have two wolves barking inside of me. The first wolf is filled with anger and hatred and bitterness and mostly revenge. The second wolf is filled with love and kindness and happiness and mostly forgiveness." The grandson looks up at his grandfather and says, "Which wolf do you think will win, Grandpa?" And the grandfather responds, "Whichever one I feed."

I think that Unity's message of being aware of the thoughts we are sending out into the world helps us make that connection. Saint Francis also understood this 800 years ago when he suggested that "where there is hatred, let me sow love; where there is injury, pardon; where there is doubt, faith; where there is despair, hope; where there is darkness, light; and where there is sadness, joy."

The words of Saint Francis offer us more than a prayer—they describe a kind of prayer technology. Everything is energy, and energy doesn't come into us in the form of good and bad and right and wrong. Energy comes as high energy and low energy. Fast energy not only nullifies slow energy, but it converts it. For instance, if we are ready to light a candle in a dark room, we do not have to warn the darkness to scurry because we are bringing light into the room. When we bring light—a higher, faster energy—into the presence of darkness, darkness is not only dissolved, but is converted into light.

When we bring the high energy of love to the presence of hatred, we are not only doing good, spiritual work, not only dissolving hatred, we are converting hatred to love. Our basic instincts are to respond to lower energies with higher energies, but we may not do that very often.

People sometimes come to me and say, "I can't really do what you practice because the people where I work have such low energy that they bring me down." Well, imagine Jesus saying, "Look, I just can't go into that place because people are too negative, and they will bring me down."

I believe that when Jesus walked into a village, his presence alone would raise the consciousness of the entire village. That's what we need to aspire to—to move to a Christlike consciousness within ourselves and respond to anger with love, rather than being angry at people for being angry at us. We can learn to do this individually in our homes, in our relationships, in our communities and also in our global world and in our cosmos.

How do we go about responding with love? Shakespeare wrote, "Go to your bosom; Knock there, and ask your heart what it doth know." When we listen to our heart, we don't act in spiritual ways because it's going to make us look good or because of any external reason. We act in spiritual ways because it's our calling. We are expressing the good that we are destined to express.

The confusion about how we go about getting along with one another happens when we hold a belief that we are separate from God. *We* separate ourselves by believing that we are what we have and what we do and what others think of us. We literally separate ourselves from our source and stop seeing ourselves as divine beings connected to God.

It's only when we let go of that way of identifying ourselves that we discover how very natural and easy it is to feel connected. We don't have to tie ourselves to others in order to be connected with them. We just have to know that, as spiritual beings, we are connected to God, to all people.

Postscript

Dr. Wayne Dyer is an internationally renowned author and speaker in the field of self-development. He is a best-selling author of 30 books, including *Your Erroneous Zones*, which was on the *New York Times* best-seller list for over a year. His latest books are *The Shift: Taking Your Life From Ambition to Meaning*, *Excuses Begone!* and *Change Your Thoughts—Change Your Life*. As a popular speaker on self-development, he has appeared on numerous radio and television shows. Dr. Dyer holds a doctorate in counseling psychology from Wayne State University (*www.drwaynedyer.com*).

On a personal note, years ago my mother had read about Dr. Dyer finding his father's grave and while there forgiving him for abandoning him soon after birth. He explained that this was a turning point in his life. Mother told me that Dr. Dyer helped her forgive her own father when he returned to reconnect with her and his seven other children after abandoning them 38 years earlier. Mother and her siblings had gone through incredible hardships without the love and support of a father during the Depression years, and yet she was able to forgive him and treat him with utmost respect. I'm sure that in forgiving her father, Mother kept her heart open to being the loving woman she was all her life. So for my mother I say, "Thank you, Dr. Dyer!

48

TRUSTING IN GOD

Trusting in God, I embrace a life filled with good.

It is not necessary for me to know how my good will come to me or when it will appear. At all times and in all ways, I trust in God for my highest good.

I open my life to that good by letting go of the past, knowing that it has no power over me. I let go of concerns about the future, releasing all of my tomorrows into God's loving care. Free from regrets about the past and free from worries about the future, I live in the present moment.

With God as my constant guide and companion, I am at peace. Just as I know that love is enfolding me, I also know this truth for those who are dear to me. God is guiding them on their right paths.

Placing my trust in God, I am ready to embrace a life filled with good!

If you abide in me, and my words abide in you, ask for whatever you wish, and it will be done for you.—John 15:7

Preview

As editor of *Daily Word*, I was most comfortable sitting behind a desk, writing and editing. One of my favorite things to do as editor was one-on-one interviews with people for *Daily Word* feature stories. Even the thought of having to speak in front of a group of people, however, caused me to feel anxious.

I've heard that some studies show that fear of public speaking ranks up there with the fear of death. At times—right when I was to speak in public—I could almost agree with that. And then one Christmas season, Rev. Christopher Chenoweth helped me begin to move beyond such fear. I found it difficult to say no to such a jovial, upbeat person as Chris when he asked me to read the *Daily Word* Christmas message at the Village Chapel. He made it sound as if this would be a most wonderful time I could ever have rather than something to dread.

At the Christmas service, I followed Jim Freeman, the poet laureate of Unity, who read one of his poems. When my turn came, I stood on stage and, looking out at the audience, I saw what Chris always saw: love shining from the faces of the Unity family who had gathered to remember and celebrate the true meaning of Christmas. Yes, I thought, this is a most wonderful experience.

In God We Trust

By Rev. Christopher Ian Chenoweth

I experienced the greatest wealth I have ever known at a time when I had only 25 cents. That's right—one shiny, new 1968 quarter.

I hadn't realized a quarter could change my life until it did, in a most dramatic way!

I had awakened that morning in a grumpy, miserable mood. I was filled with self-pity, and I flooded the air with complaints about not having enough money. "Why can't I carry a big roll of cash like some of my friends do?" I asked my wife as she came into the room. She smiled and proudly handed me a quarter that she had found on the top of the dresser.

I took a deep breath, dropped the quarter into my pocket and began complaining about having only that quarter for spending money for the whole day.

Little Did I Know

At that time I worked in broadcasting, and on this particular day, I was to do a remote broadcast from a mobile home sales lot in Baltimore, Maryland. In order for my voice to return to the radio station for signal transmission, I had to erect a high antenna. I accomplished this by putting several metal extension poles together until the antenna was the right height.

There was a strong wind blowing on this day, and I had to secure the pole so that it wouldn't wave in the wind. Being naive about such things, I assumed that the power lines suspended above me were rubber-coated; after all, birds were sitting on them and weren't being hurt. I decided that the power lines would be a convenient resting place for the antenna. Holding the pole with both hands and standing on a metal ladder, I gently placed the antenna into position, proud of the height to which I was able to raise it.

I was soon to regret my lack of knowledge, for when the metal antenna made contact with the power lines, 28,700 volts of searing electricity shot through my body. Fear gripped me. For what seemed to be an eternity (even though it was actually only five seconds), I was immobile. I could not think. The force of the electricity held me tightly; it would not let me out of its burning embrace.

Then a gust of wind blew the antenna away from the power lines. As the electricity left my body, the impact threw me away from the broadcast stage area and clear of the antenna.

I Was Alive!

Though very shaken, I was perfectly well. When a crew from the utility company arrived to investigate, they shook their heads in disbelief. Never before had they known of anyone surviving such an ordeal. The supervisor of the crew informed me that there was no logical explanation for me being able to relate the incident to them, let alone me being alive.

It was theorized that since I was holding the antenna with both hands, the full force of the electricity flowed through my chest and heart. Even the rubber tips on each leg of the ladder had melted! I should have died, yet I was very much alive and felt no pain.

A Great Discovery!

The power company insisted that I have a full medical examination, and it was at this time that the great discovery was made. On my thigh was a round first-degree burn exactly where the quarter had rested in my pocket. This was the same quarter I had so grumpily dropped in my pocket that morning.

The coin had saved my life by attracting the full force of the electricity away from the inside of my body and then shifting it to a metal part on the stage.

Embossed on the quarter are the words "In God We Trust." When I saw those words on the quarter in the hospital emergency room, I knew more about the love of God than I ever had up to that point. I knew I could trust God even when all that my human mind and eyes could perceive were lack and limitation. God is bigger than any problem. Nothing can stand up to the power of God—not even 28,700 volts of electricity.

The wealth I was given that morning years ago was more than a quarter: it was the knowledge of how God will use ordinary things and ordinary people to produce extraordinary happenings.

God gave me all I needed for that day. If there had been a large roll of paper money in my pocket, I would not be alive today. A gift was given to me that is more important than money—the gift of life.

Ever since that day, I have known that true wealth is having exactly what I need when I need it. In spite of any appearances, God has never let me down, and God will never let you down, either.

God Is Alive in Us!

Today, as a minister, I often see God working in divine, miraculous ways in people's lives. You, yourself, may have a story to tell that would cause my humble story to pale in comparison. God knows our every need; I can attest to that: I am alive today to prove it.

God is alive in you every moment to provide for your every need. No matter how great your difficulties might seem to you now, I ask you to enter into prayer and talk to God. In God, you can trust. God will pull you through anything and everything. At the very least, you will find that prayer can turn your day around positively, and maybe, as it did for me, prayer will change your life.

Postscript

Christopher Ian Chenoweth is an ordained Unity minister. He is currently serving as senior minister of *www.PositiveChristianity.org*.

Recently Chris told me that when he left his position as senior minister of the Village Chapel at Unity Village, he prayed for direction about what he was to do next. "God gave me an idea—start an online ministry—that was so foreign to my human thinking that I argued: 'I can't because I don't own a computer and have no idea how to operate one!'"

Chris went on to explain: "God knew what was right for me. I got in at the beginning of the Internet boom and became one of those .com successes that we have all heard about. Every day I send out a positive message by e-mail that goes out to people all over the world. I may not know what to do in a situation, but God does. My trust is in God."

49

MY CONSTANT COMPANION

One with God, I experience the fullness of life.

Life is filled with journeys, and some of my first journeys were learning to walk, talk, and relate to people and my environment. I am grateful for those who helped me through these passages and for the freedom to continue to grow and learn.

I also have journeys of the heart in relationships with family, friends, and even animals that come into my life. Each one helps me grow and experience the fullness of life.

The most important journey of my life is my journey with God. Moving ever forward, I satisfy the needs of my soul and understand myself and others better. I have come into a new awareness of God as my constant companion in every passage of life.

Where you go, I will go; Where you lodge, I will lodge; your people shall be my people, and your God my God.—Ruth 1:16

Preview

Considering the event of Iyanla (E-yan-la) Vanzant's birth—in the back of a Brooklyn taxi—it seems she couldn't wait to begin her journey in life. The journey of her early years, however, was difficult and even perilous at times.

As extraordinary as Iyanla's rise from poverty and seeming hopelessness is, it is her passion for helping others overcome limiting circumstances that confirms the powerful combination of prayer and faith to change what seems impossible to what is achievable in even greater ways than could be imagined.

I challenge anyone to come away from reading her story without being inspired to apply an "I can" intention to any and all circumstances of life.

Our Journeys, Our Stories

By Iyanla Vanzant

My mother passed away when I was 2, and for the next four years I was raised by my paternal grandmother, Rissie Harris. Grandmother was a Native American, and she taught me that the presence of God is in everyone and everything. She explained that we each have a responsibility to God in everything we do.

Maintaining her Native American traditions, Grandmother also embraced fundamentalist Christian teachings. Much later in life, I was able to understand that she taught me spiritual principles.

Prayer has always been an important part of my life. Grandmother was a prayer warrior in the little Pentecostal church we attended. She held the high watch during services and prayer vigils. Sometimes we would go to church on Friday evening, start praying at midnight, and continue to pray until 6 a.m. Sunday.

However, as a teenager I did what many teenagers do: I rebelled. I rebelled against the fundamentalist teachings which I found too strict and confining. By the time I was 16, I was a mother, and by age 19, I found myself in a physically abusive marriage. It wasn't until I was in my late 20s that I understood my life could be different. By then I had three children, but I was determined to finish my education and make a new life for us.

The Journey Begins

This new journey began with a slow start. Yet I had a strong foundation of spiritual teachings and prayer on which to build a new life. I just had to redefine this foundation and use it in a way that made sense in my life.

Two things hindered me for a while: I was angry with God and I was afraid of God. I was angry because my mother was dead, my father was not available, and my family was poor. I was also afraid—afraid that God was going to punish me for things I had done.

As my journey continued, however, I was relieved of that anger and fear. I began to understand that God loves me—unconditionally—and that I could have a personal relationship with God.

This understanding was awakened in me when I read the book *The Dynamic Laws of Prayer* by Catherine Ponder. It reintroduced me to spiritual principles and how they work when they are applied in daily living. I also read my *Daily Word*.

As a single mom of three, I used spiritual principles and prayed my way through law school. After earning my degree and practicing law for three years, I learned a great lesson: Power is not in what you do, but in who you are. So I decided the legal profession was not for me.

I said, "Okay, God, what do You really want me to do, because obviously it is not this!" The answer came in the form of opportunities to share information about my own journey with others.

I began teaching workshops to women who were on public assistance. Most of the women I taught came from dysfunctional homes. I shared spiritual principles with them by talking to them about faith and about trust in God—God within them. I talked to them about the power in telling the truth and the strength derived from loving yourself and other people—giving and serving not because of the rewards, but because you love it and it feels good.

It was important for *me* to believe this too, because I wasn't earning enough to support my children and myself. All my bills were overdue. One morning as I was coming down the stairs at home, I was praying and asking God, "Maybe this is what You want me to do, but how can I do it if I'm not earning a living?"

The radio was on in the living room, and just as I stepped off the bottom step, I heard Barry White, a popular singer who was being interviewed, say: "You gotta have faith. You gotta be willing to do it for free. You have to take the ups and the downs, but if you have faith and the ability, you are going to make it."

Keep on Keeping On

I knew in that moment that it was a message from God to keep doing what I was doing. I told the bill collectors, "Okay, cut the phone off; cut the lights off." Ultimately, I was evicted from my home, but my youngest daughter and I moved in with a friend. My oldest daughter had received a full four-year scholarship to college and my son had enlisted in the Navy. My girlfriends and I pooled our money to buy our meals.

Life wasn't easy, but I think that when challenges growl at us, we need to check to see if they have teeth, not just run away from them. And sometimes we have to be willing to get bitten.

Shortly after I was evicted, things started turning around. The organization where I was doing the workshops offered me a full-time job. I had written a workbook for those classes—a compilation of what my grandmother had taught me and what I had learned about my own personal, spiritual connection to God. Eventually, that compilation became my first book, *Tapping the Power Within*.

Then, with the encouragement of a friend, I started writing and doing a series of one-minute radio spots—just to get people started on a positive note in the morning. Those scripts grew into another book, titled *Acts of Faith*. When this book was published, I realized that writing—telling my story—was what God intended for me to do.

God always says *yes* to our prayers. We must, however, be conscious of what we are praying for. Since every thought, every word and every action is a prayer, we want to be conscious of everything we think, say and do, because God will always say *yes*.

My work now is rejoicing. My life is rejoicing. I am rejoicing. That doesn't mean that I never have challenges or that I have nothing to learn. What it means is that I am learning and growing and rejoicing because I have the tools I need: I have faith, and I trust God implicitly. My faith and trust in God have made my life a joyful experience—and life doesn't get much better than this.

Postscript

Iyanla Vanzant is an ordained minister, an internationally recognized spiritual teacher and a best-selling author. When Iyanla and her daughter, Gemmia, founded Inner Visions in 1998, they offered small classes that focused on ways of transforming challenging experiences into empowering lessons of victory. Inner Visions now offers multifaceted training programs with certification in Mastery of Life Skills, Life Coaching, and Ministerial Ordination. As chief executive officer of Inner Visions Worldwide, Iyanla conducts workshops and gives more than 100 public lectures annually. She is also the award-winning author of five *New York Times* best-sellers, including *Acts of Faith, One Day My Soul Just Opened Up*, and *In the Meantime*. Visit *www.innervisionsworldwide.com*.

Featured as a life coach on the NBC-TV daytime drama *Starting Over* from 2004 to 2006, Iyanla passionately delivered her special brand of self-empowerment and inspiration to others. As a standard bearer for the power of forgiveness and love to heal, she says, "Challenges come so we can grow and be prepared for things we are not equipped to handle now. When we face our challenges with faith, prepared to learn, willing to make changes, and if necessary, to let go, we are demanding our power be turned on."

50

LOVING ACTIONS

Centered in God's love, I am fulfilled.

The life I live every day is my unique and individual expression of God's love. My thoughts are formed by my belief that God is all and in all. My words are uplifting and sure. My actions are full of life and energy, and they shine with love. My intention is to be loving and life-affirming in all that I think, say and do. With the life of Jesus as my example, I serve and I love.

Each person is a child of God. Through the lens of this understanding, I see the sacredness of all people. I appreciate their contributions and treat them with compassion.

Centered in God's love, I give to life through my loving actions, and I am fulfilled. I know that I am right where I am supposed to be, doing what is mine to do.

You call me Teacher and Lord—and you are right, for that is what I am. So if I, your Lord and Teacher, have washed your feet, you also ought to wash one another's feet.
—John 13:13-14

Preview

One of the first instructions I remember my parents giving me when I was a child was this: Don't talk to or stare at strangers. Even as an adult I tried always to follow these instructions.

I don't believe that I was actually staring as I waited in an airport in San Francisco one day, but I do know that I couldn't help watching a scene (described in the following article) that was unfolding just to the left of where I was seated. Two young men and a baby brought tears to my eyes and hope to my heart. Later, on the plane, as I was walking down the aisle, I couldn't go past the young men and baby without saying something to them.

That decision led to the following story—one that to this day I feel blessed in hearing and also sharing with the *Daily Word* readers.

An Angel to Love

By Colleen Zuck

I was not quite 4 years old when rheumatic fever transformed me from a healthy, rambunctious girl, always on the move, to a bedridden child who could hardly move without a great deal of pain. To this day, I remember details of the room where I was so lovingly cared for. During the day, it was bathed in sunlight that streamed through two large, lace-curtained windows. Often when I awoke, my mother would be on her knees, beside my bed, praying for me. At any time during my recovery, I don't know that she was ever more than a few steps away from me or ever stopped praying.

As I think back, I understand how the love and faith of my parents helped me heal. Love was a balm for my painful joints as Dad lifted me from my bed to the divan so Mom could change my sheets. He was a big man—6 feet 2 inches with huge hands—but he was incredibly gentle with me, because any movement of my limbs seemed to set my joints on fire.

Recently such scenes from my childhood came to mind as I was waiting at the airport in San Francisco. From across the room, I watched a young man lift a child out of a carrier seat, as he worked around her feeding and respirator tubes. Then he held the golden-haired girl in his arms and gently kissed her forehead. I sat transfixed as I watched him use a suction machine to clear her throat while another young man accompanying him checked the monitor of her portable respirator.

Later I had an opportunity to talk with this young father, Jeremy, and learned his daughter's name was Bailey and the friend helping him was David. I was both in awe of and inspired by what Jeremy shared about his family.

A New Family

Jeremy married Earlene in 2001 and became an instant father to her 18-month-old daughter, Caitlin. Being a loving dad to Caitlin came naturally for Jeremy, and soon their family would grow to include a new baby, EmiLee.

Jeremy and Earlene brought a lot of love to their union, but didn't know until after they had lost EmiLee that they brought something else. They were both carriers of a gene that could cause a child of theirs to be born with a rare genetic disorder called spinal muscular atrophy. EmiLee succumbed to this disorder on September 22, 2003. And exactly one year later, on September 22, 2004, Bailey was born. From all appearances, she seemed healthy at birth, but within a few months, Jeremy and Earlene became concerned about her health.

When she was 6 months old—in the hospital with pneumonia—Bailey's pediatrician asked her parents: "For your own peace of mind, do you want us to test Bailey for spinal muscular atrophy?" They agreed because if she did have this disorder, they wanted Bailey to have the very best chance to survive. When the test came back positive for SMA, Jeremy and Earlene both promised never to give up on Bailey and never to give up on each other.

Earlene's aunt was surfing the Internet one day and found information on clinical trials on SMA being done at Stanford School of Medicine in California. Jeremy and Earlene called Stanford, giving them information on Bailey, and within 45 minutes, they received a call that Bailey had been accepted into Stanford's clinical trials on SMA.

The small town in Kansas where Jeremy and Earlene live is quite a distance from Stanford. This means that Jeremy and Earlene or Jeremy and family friend David take Bailey to Stanford on a commercial airline flight once a month. The clinical test that Bailey is participating in is a double-blind study. No one knows yet if the treatment she is receiving contains medicine that shows promise of strengthening her muscles or even curing SMA.

In their hearts, Jeremy and Earlene believe that Bailey is receiving the life-saving medicine because of the progress she has made. With such a severe case of SMA, Bailey was never expected to be able to talk: she now has a vocabulary of about 75 words and speaks with clarity and volume. One of her nurses is also teaching her sign language. Bailey was never expected to be able to move her shoulders and arms enough to put her hands above her head: she does that now. She is also holding her head up by herself for short periods of time. The movement in her legs has improved, and Bailey delights in kicking her feet to set off alarms, sending the monitors on her machines into a tailspin.

Prayer has been and continues to be an important part of Bailey's recovery. Family members and friends are believing in a miracle for her. I invite you to hold Bailey and all the children of our world who need healing in your prayers.

Seeing Bailey and her father that day at the airport remains a precious memory for me. And so does what Jeremy said when I asked him how he and Earlene find the strength to do all that they do in such a committed and loving way.

He paused for a moment and then said: "We have each other, we have our family, and we have her. Waking up in the morning and hearing Bailey talk and play—that right there is enough."

As if God had sent them their own special angel to love, Jeremy and Earlene go about tenderly caring for Bailey. This is what the love of this young couple so beautifully demonstrates to me—a love that is quiet and unyielding because of the incredible depths from which it flows.

Postscript

So often after I have read or heard about people who are going through a challenge, I wish I could learn how they are currently doing.

A year or so after I had met Jeremy and Bailey at the airport, I decided to contact Jeremy. I have to admit, I had a bit of reservation about making the call. I wanted to hear nothing but *good* news. It took several calls in which I left messages on his answering machine before Jeremy called me. When he did, I braced myself for an answer when I asked: "How is Bailey doing?"

He did have good news to share. Bailey had continued to improve. She was still taking part in the clinical trails for SMA, and Jeremy and Earlene hadn't been told if she was receiving life-saving medicine in the double-blind study. What they did know was that she was getting better, and that was what mattered the most.

I still think of this family, and each time I do, I hold a picture in mind of a blond, curly-headed child. I like to think that my thoughts are prayers for a special little angel called Bailey.

Colleen first visited Unity Village as a teen with a friend and her family. "We stayed in one of the cabins for a weekend," she says, "and on a walk in Unity's apple orchard, my friend and I picked one apple each. We were convinced that a couple of apples would never be missed from the apple-laden trees of the orchard. I have always felt a tinge of guilt about not asking permission to pick that apple, but in all my years of eating apples, I remember that one to be the juiciest, sweetest apple I have ever tasted. I like to think that in my 40 years of service at Unity, I somehow made restitution for the purloined apple."

"I came to work at Unity because I needed to support my two-year-old son and myself," she says. "Unity became more than a place to earn a living. At Unity and through the teachings, I discovered friends and a way of life that have supported me in the most challenging and rewarding times of my life."

When Colleen married Bill, she inherited four beautiful daughters, which delighted her son John, who thought that being an only child was "not fair." Colleen and Bill now have 10 grandchildren and two great-grandchildren. She and Bill have had several "pets" on their five-acres of land in Raymore, Missouri: a pot-bellied pig, a goat, sheep, and several dogs. "We have downsized in our retirement years," she says. "Currently we have only two miniature horses and two dogs."

"When I first came to Unity, I was befriended by Stahr Pope," she says, "and Stahr told me something that enriched every day of my experience as an employee and in life itself: 'Colleen, in reality, you are not working for Unity; you are working for God, knowing this, you will always find joy in what you do.' How true this is. God is so good."

Printed in U.S.A.

B0019